Desserts and Jams

Madame Benoit

Encyclopedia of microwave cooking

micro wave

Desserts and Jams

Héritage plus

Front cover design: Bouvry Designer Inc.
Front cover and inside photography: Paul Casavant
Conception and research: Marie-Christine Payette
Dishes loaned by courtesy of: Le Curio, Montenach Mall, Beloeil.
Cover: Strawberry shortcake (recipe p. 57)

Legal Deposit: 3rd quarter 1986
Bibliothèque nationale du Québec
National Library of Canada

ISBN: 2-7625-5811-5   Printed in Canada

LES ÉDITIONS HÉRITAGE INC.
300, Arran, Saint-Lambert, Quebec J4R 1K5
(514) 672-6710

Table of Contents

Foreword

Desserts are not "passé"

Some say that desserts are old fashioned and "passé"; others refuse them categorically. . . they are dieting!

The one subject on which any group of gourmets, epicures or just about anyone will immediately fly to verbal arms is "Dessert versus no desserts". Oddly enough, desserts usually are the winners, especially with men. Truly sincere dessert abstainers are few and the others are silently envious when they look at the many delectable elegant sweets.

When I say delectable and elegant, I wonder if it conveys the feeling that it might be difficult and tedious to prepare such desserts. The answer is no, and doubly no, when the microwave oven is used. For example, there is no way to know the true flavor of a poached fruit without tasting it poached in the microwave oven.

Throughout this book I will discuss cakes, pies, muffins, creams, mousses, cold or hot soufflés, poached fruits, jams, etc., all of these from the simple to the dramatic, yet all quick and easy with the microwave cooking method.

I admit some desserts will need to be cooked by the convection method of the microwave oven. . . and why not!

Introduction

Many people have said to me: "I would not have the patience to change all my recipes", and so, I have decided to write this Encyclopedia of Microwave Cooking, so that you may realize how easy this method is once understood.

Microwave cooking is equally convenient for the small family with everyone working outside, as it is for the large family where larger servings are needed. All that's needed is knowing how to proceed.

How does a microwave cook?

When you know the basic facts about the way a microwave oven works, you will find it easy even when using it for the first few times.

Microwaves are somewhat like radio-frequency waves. The radio frequency waves are called "Microwaves" because they are very short in length. When the microwaves enter any food containing water molecules, these are activated and move about so rapidly that they hit and rub against other molecules in the food, producing heat by friction at the molecular level. This is what produces great heat so quickly in food cooked in a microwave oven.

How does the "Convection" part of a microwave oven work?

Simply like any other classic type of oven.
Example: Preheat oven to 350°F. (180°C) 15 minutes.
        Bake 40 minutes at 350°F. (180°C).
Look for pad indicating the above and proceed to enter the required temperature and time just as for any type of electric oven.

Why do we often refer to Microwaving as "cool cooking"?

Because if a cup is filled with boiling water, the cup will pick up some of the heat from the water. The oven also picks up some heat from the food cooking in it, but very little since after prolonged cooking, the walls of the oven will be cool enough to touch. Also, a cooking container does not get hotter than the food that is cooking in it, but a covered container will get hotter than an uncovered one, because the steam produced by the cooking is trapped in it. Some think that microwaves stay in the food being cooked.

Absolutely not, they don't. They act like light rays — when a light is turned on, the room becomes lit by the rays, but as soon as the switch is turned off, the electricity ceases to exist.

The same thing is true of microwave ovens: the waves exist only while the magnetron tube is turned on, and microwaves cannot remain in the food any more than light rays can be stored in the room.

How does heat penetration work?

First, microwaves do not cook food from the inside out, but as microwaves penetrate the surface of foods, many are "absorbed" by the first water molecules and instantly change into heat. Many of the microwaves that go beyond the surface are "absorbed" by water molecules just below the surface. The heat that is generated by the microwaves must then reach the center of the food by conduction, which is a very slow process. That is why the recipes often ask to stir a food or a sauce as it helps to distribute the heat evenly throughout the food being cooked plus allowing quicker and more even cooking.

The importance of knowing your oven

There are many models of microwave ovens, even of the same brand. It is therefore of utmost importance to become well acquainted with your oven, and to know and understand all its features.

What to do
- Once the oven is plugged in, place a bowl of water in it, close the door, and read the operation manual following every step as suggested.
Example: Heat oven at HIGH for 2 minutes.

Look for Power Select HIGH and program, then look for the START setting; touch to put the oven on. You will then understand how this operation works.

Repeat this procedure for all types of operations, and very soon you will realize how easy it is, and you will understand how your own oven works.

Be Knowledgeable About Microwave Terms
There are many brands of microwave ovens on the market. That is why it is important to understand the language. Read and learn the following notes and microwave cooking will become clear and easy.

Rotate
If your oven has a turntable or a special system, such as Rotaflow, multiflow or any other hidden turntable that does the same work as the rotating type, then you do not have to rotate the dish in which the food is cooking. Otherwise, give a quarter turn to the dish one or twice during the cooking period.

Let Stand
Many recipes read "Let stand x minutes after cooking". Since the microwave process of cooking is actually intense molecular vibration, food continues to cook even after the microwave energy is turned off. In a way, the same happens when food is cooked in x time in an ordinary oven and we let it stand. With microwaves the standing time lets the molecules come to rest. This is just like a bouncing ball that dribbles down to a gradual stopping point. It is often referred to as "aftercook".

When a recipe says "Let stand x minutes, stir and serve," that is exactly what is meant.

High or Full Power
This means a continuous cycle with maximum (100%) output, whatever your brand of oven.
The recipes in each volume of this encyclopedia were prepared for microwave ovens with wattage in the 650 - 700 range. If your oven has a lower output, increase the cooking time slightly according to the conversion chart.

```
┌──────────────────── IMPORTANT ────────────────────┐
│                                                     │
│                                                     │
│      The following recipes were tested in 650-700   │
│   watt microwave ovens.                             │
│                                                     │
│      Lower-wattage ovens may necessitate some       │
│   adjustment in timing.                             │
│                                                     │
│      The recipes in general will serve 6 medium     │
│   portions or 4 large portions.                     │
│                                                     │
└─────────────────────────────────────────────────────┘
```

650-700W	500-600W	400-500W
15 seconds	18 seconds	21 seconds
30 seconds	36 seconds	42 seconds
45 seconds	54 seconds	1 minute
1 minute	1 min 10 sec.	1 min 25 sec.
2 minutes	2 min 30 sec.	2 min 45 sec.
3 minutes	3 min 30 sec.	4 minutes
4 minutes	4 min 45 sec.	5 min 30 sec.
5 minutes	6 minutes	7 minutes
6 minutes	7 min 15 sec.	8 min 25 sec.
7 minutes	8 min 25 sec.	9 min 45 sec.
8 minutes	9 min 30 sec.	11 minutes
9 minutes	10 min 45 sec.	12 min 30 sec.
10 minutes	12 minutes	14 minutes
15 minutes	18 minutes	20 minutes
20 minutes	24 minutes	27 minutes
25 minutes	30 minutes	34 minutes
30 minutes	36 minutes	41 minutes

This chart gives you an idea of the time needed for any food you cook in an oven with the above wattage.
However, it is always wise, regardless of wattage, to check the cooking when 2 minutes of the cooking period still remain. That's assuming, of course, that the cooking time indicated is over 2 minutes.

Power Level Chart

Power	Output	Use
HIGH	100% .... (700 watts)	Boil water Brown ground meat Cook fresh fruits and vegetables Cook fish Cook poultry (up to 3 lb [1.5 kg]) Heat beverages (not containing milk) Make candy Preheat Browning Dish (accessory)
M. HIGH	90% .... (650 watts)	Heat frozen foods (not containing eggs or cheese) Heat canned foods Reheat leftovers Warm baby food
MEDIUM	70% .... (490 watts)	Bake cakes Cook meats Cook shellfish Prepare eggs and delicate food
M. LOW	50% .... (360 watts)	Bake muffins Cook custards Melt butter and chocolate Prepare rice
LOW	27% .... (200 watts)	Less tender cuts of meat Simmer stews and soups Soften butter and cheese
WARM	10% .... (70 watts)	Keep foods at serving temperature Rise yeast breads Soften ice cream
"Defrost"	35% .... (245 watts)	All thawing, see Defrosting Charts
"Delay Stand"	0% .... (0 watts)	Start heating at later time Program stand time after cooking

IMPI — International Microwave Power Institute — is an international institution governing microwave data throughout the world for kitchens, hospitals, etc.
IMPI have set the standards which have been adopted with regard to the designation of Power Settings for Microwave Ovens: HIGH, MEDIUM-HIGH, MEDIUM, MEDIUM-LOW, LOW, REHEAT, DEFROST, START, which must be observed everywhere in the world.

Variable Power

This describes the choice of power levels that allow you to prepare food in the microwave which normally would be over sensitive to continuous microwave activity. To easily understand this process, it is actually an "on and off" cycle timed for varying amounts of microwave energy, which means that this pulsating action effectively creates slower cooking activity, without your having to worry about it. If your recipe calls for 1/2 power, this equals MEDIUM-SLOW, which is like constant simmering.

When microwave cooking first began, ovens had only "Cook" and "Defrost" cycles. Some of you may still have these ovens, so remember that you effectively "simmer" on the Defrost cycle or whenever 1/2 power or MEDIUM is called for. For all other cooking, use the Cook cycle and add a few minutes to the cooking period called for in the recipe.

There are many other ways to cook in the various microwave ovens, so always be ready to give serious attention to your oven manual, and you will soon find it is all very easy.

What influences microwave oven cooking period

Three factors have a major influence on microwave oven cooking times.

A. **The starting temperature,** which influences the total cooking time. The colder the food, the longer it must cook.

B. **The density of the food** affects its cooking time. A bread roll being lightweight and porous will cook much faster than a dense food, such as carrots and potatoes, etc.

C. **The total amount of food** cooking in the oven at the same time affects the cooking time more than any other factor.

If the quantity of food being cooked is doubled, and as there are no fast rules as to how to increase the cooking period, when in doubt check once or twice during the cooking period.

For example: Two slices of bacon will cook in a minute or two, but 4 slices of bacon could take 3 to 4 minutes.

Stirring, once or twice, will shorten the cooking period. Heat is generated in the outer layers of the food and then must reach the center by conduction.

How to arrange food in the microwave

It is important to remember that food cooks more quickly at the outer edge of the container. Also, it cooks more slowly in the center of the dish. Place the largest or densest or thickest part of any piece of food toward the outer edge of the plate. Place thinner or small pieces in the center. This way it will even out the irregularly shaped pieces of food. For instance, irregularly shaped potatoes are best placed spoke-fashion with the smaller end toward the middle and the large end out. Cover the food to be reheated with a piece of waxed paper.

What is "Conduction" Heat

Conduction heat is a slow way for heat to travel through food. By stirring, cold food from the center of the food mass is brought to the surface to be heated and hot food from the surface is taken to the center. This, when necessary, evens out the heat.

Example: We could not stir a cake or a pie, which do not require stirring, but we could stir poached fresh fruits or sweet sauces, etc.

Residual Cooking

- Another fact important to know, understand and remember — that is the residual cooking which takes place in the food after it is removed from the microwave oven. The heavier and denser a piece of food, such as a roast, the more residual cooking takes place. So we must always remember that in microwave cooking there is a greater amount of residual cooking than in conventional cooking. For example: we can microwave an 8-inch (20 cm) cake in 3 minutes, but it will take the cake 8 to 10 minutes on the counter to attain its perfect texture.
- Another very important point, during the period of microwave cooking water molecules gain momentum, and it takes time for that momentum to be used, even after the microwave oven stops cooking and the cooked food is placed on a table. While this momentum is being used by the food, more cooking occurs because more heat continues to be produced. This is an important fact to remember so your food will never be overcooked.

Standing time

This is one of the most important points to remember in microwave cooking.
It is the time needed in many foods between the point at which they are taken from the microwave oven to the point at which they are served. This is an important moment, which is needed to allow residual cooking to take place.
The heavier and denser a food, the more standing time is needed.
Example: a cake needs less standing time than a pie.

Degree of Moisture in Food

(1) The degree of moisture in food:
   the higher it is: faster and shorter cooking period;
   the lower it is: slower and longer cooking period.
(2) The quantity of liquid added to the food:
   the greater the quantity, the longer the cooking period will be.
(3) The density of produce:
   Porous = faster cooking: tomatoes, spinach, mushrooms, etc.
   More dense = longer cooking: peas, cauliflower, etc.
(4) Room temperature is the ideal temperature to start cooking:
   Fresh picked from the garden or at room temperature: faster cooking.
   Colder temperature: food taken from refrigerator or after thawing : longer cooking.
(5) The structure of the food:
   Smaller pieces = faster cooking: a small potato.
   Larger pieces = longer cooking: a large potato.
(6) Certain foods are covered during the cooking period, as indicated in the recipe, to prevent the natural moisture from evaporating.
(7) The degree of sugar content determines the degree of heat produced:
   The more sugar, the more intense the heat and the shorter the cooking period: syrup, caramel, etc.
(8) The more fat in food, the faster it will cook.
(9) The arrangement of the food plays an important role:
   4 to 5 potatoes placed in a circle will cook faster than if they were simply placed in the oven.

Degree of moisture - adding of water - density - thickness - structure - covers - amount of sugar - degree of fat - arrangement of food - appropriate accessories - are all key words relating your cooking to the factors of heat, weight and temperature.

How food is cooked in the Microwave Oven

Microwaves are a form of high frequency radio wave similar to those used by a radio including AM, FM, and CB.

Electricity is converted into microwave energy by the magnetron tube, and microwaves are approximately four to six inches (10 to 15 cm) long with a diameter of about one-fourth inch (6mm). From the magnetron tube, microwave energy is transmitted to the oven cavity where it is: reflected, transmitted and absorbed.

Reflection

Microwaves are reflected by metal just as a ball is bounced off a wall. That is why the inside of the oven is metal covered with epoxy. A combination of stationary (interior walls) and rotating metal (turntable or stirrer fan) helps assure that the microwaves are well distributed within the oven cavity to produce even cooking.

Transmission

Microwaves pass through some materials such as paper, glass and plastic much like sunlight shining through a window. Because these substances do not absorb or reflect the microwave energy, they are ideal materials for microwave oven cooking containers.

Absorption

During heating, microwaves will be absorbed by food. They penetrate to a depth of about 3/4 to 1½ inches (2 to 4 cm). Microwave energy excites the molecules in the food (especially wate and sugar molecules), and causes them to vibrate at a rate of 2,450,000,000 times per second. Thi vibration causes friction, and heat is produced. If you vigorously rub your hands together, you w heat produced by friction. The internal cooking is then done by conduction. **The heat** which is produced by friction is conducted to the center of the food.

Foods also continue to cook by conduction during standing time, which keeps the cooked food warm for 4 to 10 minutes after cooking, and makes it possible to cook 3 to 4 dishes with only one oven, and to serve everything warm.

How to cook a complete meal in the Microwave Oven

If your menu calls for a roast, potatoes and green peas, cook the roast first. During its waiting period, cook the potatoes, they will remain warm from 20 to 30 minutes covered with a cloth, then the vegetable with the shortest cooking period.

The dessert may be cooked before the meat, or if it is to be served hot, cook it during the meal and let it stand in the oven. The oven goes off when the bell rings, and the food may be left inside until it is time to serve it.

The best containers to use in the Microwave Oven

Many types of containers can be used in the microwave oven.

Glass — Most of you have Pyrex or Corningware. They all go in the microwave oven and are also attractive to take from the oven to the table.

Plastic — There are two types of plastic: the soft and semi-soft, but very often the Melamine or soft type cracks, warps or blisters in the microwave oven.

The other type of plastic will not crack or warp from the effects of the microwaves, but care should be taken when using it because often this plastic will pick up heat from the food which can warp or soften the plastic.

That is why I recommend the "Micro-Dur" type of plastic dish, they are the perfect type of plastic dishes to cook with, and even the cover can be used. Their plus is that plastic paper is not needed when cooking by Sensor or any method that calls for a plastic covering, as the cover does the work and it is surely more economical. They are not to be used when cooking by the Convection Method.
Another brand of plastic ware, "Micro-Mac", is also very good. The same rules as above should be followed, except for the cover.

Glass Measuring cups
There are five sizes in the glass measuring cups: 1 cup (250 mL), 2 cups (500 mL), 3 cups (750 mL), 4 cups (1 L) and 8 cups (2 L). The 8-cup is not so readily available, but I find it most useful and well worth looking for.

Magnetic Turntable

Some ovens are equipped with an automatic magnetic turntable or a small fan in the top of the oven, or an invisible rotating system (whichever is featured in your Microwave, will be explained in your instruction manual), then you do not have to rotate the dish.
If your Microwave has neither turntable, nor fan, nor invisible rotating system, then you will have to rotate the dish for even cooking as the Microwave may tend to focus more on a definite spot in the food, especially if there is fat in the meat, and remember that they are not always visible. What happens is that the fat parts cook more quickly because the reflection area is not altered, so, of course the cooking dish may be rotated.

How to reheat cooked food in the Microwave Oven

A single pie portion: Set the piece of pie on a plate, reheat at MEDIUM-HIGH, 1 to 1½ minutes, according to thickness of the filling. Let stand 1 minute.
Doughnuts: 1 doughnut — 15 seconds at MEDIUM-HIGH.
            2 doughnuts — 20 to 30 seconds at MEDIUM-HIGH
            3 doughnuts — 1 minute or a little less
Rolls: Wrap in a white kitchen paper
       2 rolls — 15 to 16 seconds at MEDIUM-HIGH
       4 rolls — 20 to 30 seconds at MEDIUM-HIGH
Beware of overheating any of these, including a square of baked cake which will be hot in 15 seconds, always at MEDIUM-HIGH.
For any cooked foods I wish to warm up, I use MEDIUM-HIGH. When I am not sure of the time, I start with 15 seconds and add slowly what is needed.
It is a very good rule to let warmed up food stand for 1/2 to 1 minute before serving.
To reheat a plate of meat and vegetables, cover food with waxed paper and reheat at MEDIUM-HIGH from 1 to 2½ minutes, depending on the quantity. Let stand 1 minute before serving.
Another exciting factor when reheating food in the microwave oven is that it tastes fresh-cooked.

Introduction to Metric Measures

Millillitre (mL): replaces the fluid ounce
Litre (L): replaces the quart
Gram (g): replaces the ounce
Kilogram (kg): replaces the pound
Degrees Celsium (°C): replaces
  degrees Fahrenheit
Centimetre (cm): replaces the inch

250 mL	replaces an 8-ounce cup
15 mL	replaces 1 tablespoon
5 mL	replaces 1 teaspoon
1 kg	a little more than 2 pounds
500 g	a little more than 1 pound
100°C	water boils
5 cm	about 2 inchs

Metric Equivalents of Most Used Measures in Cooking

Teaspoon:

1/4 teaspoon	1 mL
1/2 teaspoon	2 mL
1 teaspoon	5 mL
2 teaspoon	10 mL

Tablespoon:

1 tablespoon	15 mL
2 tablespoon	30 mL
3 tablespoon	50 mL
4 tablespoon	60 mL
2 to 3 tablespoon	30 à 50 mL
4 to 6 tablespoon	60 à 90 mL

Cups:

1/4 cup	60 mL
1/3 cup	80 mL
1/2 cup	125 mL
3/4 cup	190 mL
1 cup	250 mL
1¼ cups	315 mL
1⅓ cups	330 mL
1½ cups	375 mL
2 cups	500 mL
3 cups	750 mL
4 cups	1 L
5 cups	1.25 L
6 cups	1.5 L

Temperatures

150°F	65°C
200°F	95°C
250°F	120°C
300°F	150°C
350°F	180°C
400°F	200°C
425°F	225°C
450°F	230°C
500°F	260°C

Cold Lemon Soufflé (p. 19) →

Snow Eggs (photo opposite)

An old-fashioned dessert made the world over, sometimes caramelized when an elegant dessert is desired; but believe me, it is very good without the caramel.

1½ cups (375 mL) milk

1/2 cup (125 mL) light cream

1/4 cup (60 mL) sugar

1 tsp. (5 mL) vanilla

2 egg whites

1/4 cup (60 mL) sugar

A pinch of salt

1/2 tsp. (2 mL) vanilla

3 egg yolks

Place in a 6-cup (1.5 L) ceramic dish (Corning), the milk, cream and the first 1/4 cup (60 mL) sugar. Mix well. Microwave 5 minutes at MEDIUM-HIGH, or until milk boils. Add the 1 teaspoon (5 mL) vanilla. Beat egg whites with the remaining sugar and a pinch of salt until stiff. Add the 1/2 teaspoon (2 mL) vanilla. Drop 6 to 8 tablespoons of the mixture into the boiling milk to form 6 to 8 mounds. Microwave uncovered 2 minutes at MEDIUM-HIGH. Turn meringue over and microwave at MEDIUM-HIGH another 30 seconds. Remove meringue from the milk with a slotted spoon into the serving dish, if necessary repeat until all the egg white is cooked.

To the remaining milk add the well beaten egg yolks, microwave at MEDIUM 2 to 3 minutes, stirring well after each minute. You should have a light creamy golden sauce. Beware of overcooking as the sauce would curdle. Stir well and pour over the cooked egg whites. Cool, then refrigerate. It may be served warm.

Maple Syrup Parfait

A quick and easy way to prepare a parfait with 2 cups (500 mL) of vanilla ice cream.

2 cups (500 mL) vanilla ice cream

2 egg yolks

1/2 cup (125 mL) maple syrup

1/4 cup (60 mL) chopped nuts (optional)

2 egg whites

1/2 tsp. (2 mL) salt

Uncover the ice cream and let it soften at room temperature. Beat the egg yolks, gradually add the maple syrup while beating. Microwave 2 minutes at MEDIUM. Stir well and microwave 1 more minute at MEDIUM. Stir again. The sauce should be smooth and creamy. Cool, add to the softened ice cream together with the nuts. Stir well. An electric beater may be used.

Beat the egg whites stiff with the salt. Fold into the ice cream. Pour into a mold. Cover and refrigerate 4 to 5 hours before serving.

← **Top: Snow Eggs (recipe above)**
← **Center: Dover Chocolate Pudding (p. 19)**
← **Bottom: Red Wine Jelly (p. 23)**

Nassau Chocolate Mousse

Serve in small cups or as a pie filling with chocolate cookie crumb crust.

2 squares (1 oz (24 g) each) semi-sweet
    chocolate

1/3 cup (80 mL) vanilla or plain white sugar

1 envelope unflavored gelatine

3 egg yolks

A pinch of salt

1 cup (250 mL) milk

3 tbsp. (50 mL) rum or brandy

3 egg whites

1/3 cup (80 mL) sugar

1 cup (250 mL) whipping cream

Melt the chocolate in a bowl 2 minutes at MEDIUM-HIGH. Add the first 1/3 cup (80 mL) sugar and the gelatine, stir. Beat in the egg yolks and salt, stir in the milk and rum or brandy, mix well. Microwave 4 minutes at HIGH, or until mixture is slightly thickened, stirring 3 times during the cooking period. Cool 30 to 40 minutes.

Beat the egg whites until foamy, gradually add the other 1/3 cup (80 mL) sugar and beat until stiff. Fold this meringue into the cold chocolate cream.

Whip the cream until stiff and fold the chocolate mixture into it. Spoon into 6 to 8 individual dessert cups or into an 8-inch (20 cm) crumb or cookie crust. Refrigerate 3 to 12 hours.

Lemon Mousse

An elegant, light cool dessert to serve in the heat of summer, or any time throughout the year after a rich meal.

1/2 cup (125 mL) sugar

1 envelope unflavored gelatine

1/4 tsp. (1 mL) salt

1/2 cup (125 mL) water

1/2 cup (125 mL) lemon juice

The grated rind of 1 lemon

3 eggs, separated

1/3 cup (80 mL) sugar

1 cup (250 mL) whipping cream

Mix together in a 4-cup (1 L) bowl the sugar, gelatine, salt, water, lemon juice and rind.

Beat the egg yolks and add to the mixture. Microwave uncovered 2 minutes at MEDIUM-HIGH, stir well. Microwave 2 more minutes at MEDIUM-HIGH, stir again. If necessary, microwave another 2 minutes. Cool for mixture to thicken, about 30 minutes.

Beat the egg whites until frothy, beat in the remaining 1/3 cup (80 mL) sugar and fold into the cooled lemon mixture. Whip cream and also fold into mixture.

Pour into an attractive serving bowl of your choice. Refrigerate 6 to 12 hours or until ready to serve.

Cold Lemon Soufflé (photo opposite p. 16)

Super served with lightly sweetened strawberries or raspberries. But you can also cover and place in the freezer for 12 hours to obtain a frozen soufflé.

3 egg yolks

1 cup (250 mL) sugar

1 envelope unflavored gelatine

1/4 cup (60 mL) cold water

1/3 cup (80 mL) fresh lemon juice

Grated rind of 1 lemon

1½ cups (375 mL) whipping cream

3 egg whites, beaten

Beat egg yolks until pale yellow, add the sugar gradually, beating thoroughly. The mixture will then be light and creamy.

Soak the gelatine 2 minutes in the cold water. Add the fresh lemon juice and rind to the egg yolk mixture.

Microwave the gelatine 30 seconds at HIGH, add to the creamed mixture, stirring as it is added. Stir to mix thoroughly. Refrigerate until mixture has the texture of egg whites.

Whip the cream, beat the egg whites and gradually add both to the lemon mixture. Pour into a serving dish. Refrigerate 2 hours before serving. It can be refrigerated 2 to 3 days before being served.

Dover Chocolate Pudding (photo opposite p. 17, center)

No one will dare call this very interesting English dessert a bread pudding.

3 tbsp. (50 mL) butter

1 1-oz (28 g) unsweetened chocolate

1/2 cup (125 mL) sugar

3 eggs

1 cup (250 mL) light cream or milk

1½ cups (375 mL) soft white breadcrumbs

1/4 cup (60 mL) slivered toasted almonds

Place the butter and unsweetened chocolate in a bowl, microwave 2 minutes at MEDIUM-HIGH, stirring once. When chocolate is melted add the sugar and stir until well mixed. Beat the eggs until fluffy. Add to chocolate mixture while stirring, add the cream or milk and stir to mix thoroughly. Microwave 2 minutes at HIGH, stirring once, if needed, it could be microwaved 40 seconds more, the difference depends on how cold the cream or milk was. When creamy, let stand a few minutes, stir in the breadcrumbs. Microwave uncovered 2 minutes at HIGH. Let stand 15 minutes before serving. Sprinkle the toasted almonds on top.

Pulled Bread Chocolate Pudding

The fact that the bread is pulled from the soft center part in small pieces gives an almost soufflé texture to this bread pudding.

2 cups (500 mL) milk or light cream	1/2 tsp. (2 mL) salt
4 to 5 slices fresh white bread	1/4 cup (60 mL) butter
1/3 cup (80 mL) unsweetened cocoa	2 eggs, well beaten
1/2 cup (125 mL) brown sugar	1 tsp. (5 mL) vanilla

Pour the milk or light cream into a bowl, microwave 5 minutes at HIGH. Remove crust from bread and pull the white soft bread into small pieces. Pour the hot milk on top, let cool to tepid.
Mix the cocoa, brown sugar and salt. Add to the softened bread and stir until well mixed. Melt the butter 2 minutes at HIGH. Add to the bread mixture. Stir well. Beat the eggs with the vanilla. Add to the bread. Mix well. Pour into a microwave-safe serving dish. Microwave 6 minutes at MEDIUM-HIGH. Let stand 10 minutes in the microwave oven. Test for doneness with the point of a knife. If middle is still a bit uncooked, microwave 1 minute at HIGH. Let stand until just tepid.
Serve as is or with plain cream or whipped cream.

Custard with jam

If you wish to make a dessert in a jiffy with ingredients usually on hand in any kitchen, try this one. The cooking period varies depending on how cold the milk and eggs are, so make sure to check doneness after 6 minutes.

1¾ cups (440 mL) milk	1/2 tsp. (2 mL) vanilla
1/4 cup (60 mL) sugar	1/3 tsp. (.05 mL) nutmeg
3 eggs	Jam of your choice
1/4 tsp. (1 mL) salt	

Place all the ingredients, except the jam, in a 4-cup (1 L) measure or bowl. Stir well.
Pour into a Pyrex or ceramic pie plate. Microwave 6 to 9 minutes at MEDIUM-HIGH.
Let stand 5 minutes, cover with the chosen jam and serve.

Homemade Pudding Mix

This is a very handy mix to have. You are then ready at any time to prepare an economical and delicious dessert in less than five minutes. The flavoring is left to you according to your taste.

2½ cups (625 mL) powdered milk

1 cup (250 mL) sugar

3/4 cup (190 mL) cornstarch

1 tsp. (5 mL) salt

For a Chocolate Pudding Mix, *add*

3/4 cup (190 mL) unsweetened cocoa

1 tsp. (5 mL) instant coffee

Place all the ingredients in a bowl and mix thoroughly. Place in a container or a plastic bag and close tightly. Keep in a cool place. You do not have to refrigerate the mix. It keeps for 3 to 4 months.

To make a pudding:

3/4 cup (190 mL) of the basic mix

1 cup (250 mL) water

1/4 cup (60 mL) milk or cream

Place all the ingredients in a 4-cup (1 L) measuring cup. Mix and microwave 4 minutes at HIGH, stirring twice during the cooking.
To flavor, add one of the following to the cooked pudding:

1 tsp. (5 mL) vanilla

Rind of one orange or lemon OR
   2 tbsp. (30 mL) rum or brandy

Variation:
Caramel Pudding: Replace the sugar in the basic recipe with an equal quantity of brown sugar, i.e. 1 cup (250 mL). Add 1/4 tsp. (1 mL) cinnamon.
Proceed same as to make a pudding.

Helpful Hint

To soften or flavor candied fruits or raisins required in a fruit cake recipe or other.
Place in a bowl the fruits or raisins required in the recipe, pour over the liquor or other liquid as called for. Microwave 2 minutes at MEDIUM-HIGH. Cool before using.

Omelette Tropicale

This is a very easy dessert to prepare. It can be made with as many or as few eggs as you wish and the remaining ingredients are easily increased or decreased according to your needs.

1 banana, peeled and sliced	**3 eggs**
2 tbsp. (30 mL) rum	**1 tbsp. (15 mL) sugar**
1 tbsp. (15 mL) butter	**3 tbsp. (50 mL) cold water**
1 tsp. (5 mL) slivered almonds	**1 tbsp. (15 mL) currant jelly**

Soak sliced banana in rum 1 hour before making the omelette. Melt the butter in a pie plate 30 seconds at HIGH. Add the almonds, microwave 30 to 60 seconds or until golden brown, stirring once. Beat the eggs with the sugar and cold water. Pour over the almonds, microwave at MEDIUM-HIGH 1 or 2 minutes; depending on number of eggs used, cooking time may range from 30 seconds to 3 minutes.
Place the currant jelly in the middle, fold the omelette over. Pour the cold rum bananas on top. Enjoy!

Zabaglione (photo opposite p. 33, left)

The most delicate and exciting of all the Italian desserts. To make it to perfection, you must follow the instructions exactly as given. I like to make this in front of my guests, with the microwave oven set on a rolling table in the dining room.

6 egg yolks
1/4 cup (60 mL) fine granulated sugar
1/2 cup (125 mL) Marsala or Port wine

Beat the egg yolks and the sugar with an electric beater until thick and yellow. Slowly add the wine while beating all the time. I add a full tablespoon (15 mL) at a time.
Microwave, uncovered, 30 seconds at MEDIUM, then beat mixture again with electric beater until smooth and frothy. Repeat this operation twice more, beating well each time, then microwave again at MEDIUM for 15 seconds. This foamy, delicate cream should now be ready to serve, but depending on the starting temperature of the eggs, it could require another 15 seconds of cooking at MEDIUM. Pour into individual glasses. Serve hot with small meringues or just by itself.

Red Wine Jelly (photo opposite p. 17, bottom)

A cool dessert that can be made a day or two ahead of time. Serve it plain, if you wish. In the summer, I like to serve it with sweetened raspberries or whipped cream or plain cream.

1 envelope unflavored gelatine	1/2 cup (125 mL) sugar
1/4 cup (60 mL) cold water	1 cup (250 mL) jam of your choice
2 pieces of lemon peel	1 cup (250 mL) dry red wine
1 cup (250 mL) water	2 tbsp. (30 mL) brandy or lemon juice

Soak gelatine in the cold water, for 5 minutes.
Place in a bowl, the lemon peel, water, sugar and jam. Microwave 5 minutes at HIGH, stir well. Microwave 2 minutes at MEDIUM. Stir well. Add the gelatine and stir until it is dissolved. Add the remaining ingredients. Stir well. Pour into a mold (as it may be molded) or into a glass dish. Refrigerate 12 hours.

Helpful Hint

To prepare croutons or breadcrumbs, place 2 cups (500 mL) of bread cubes in a pie plate and microwave 3 to 4 minutes at HIGH, stirring a few times. To make breadcrumbs, let bread cubes cool and put through food processor to obtain the required texture.

Apples "Normandes"

Simple apple dessert. The topping of apricot or plum jam and sherry gives it a very special "something".

5 medium-sized apples	**1/4 cup (60 mL) apple juice or water**
Juice and grated rind of 1 lemon	**2 tbsp. (30 mL) apricot or plum jam**
3/4 cup (190 mL) sugar	**2 tbsp. (30 mL) sherry**

It is advisable to choose apples of equal size. Peel and cut into quarters, stir with the lemon juice.
Place the sugar and apple juice or water in a large pie plate or a 12 x 8-inch (30 x 20 cm) baking dish. Microwave 5 minutes at HIGH, stirring once.
Stir in the apples and juice, add the lemon rind. Microwave at HIGH 6 to 8 minutes, stirring once after 4 minutes to check cooking. Be careful not to overcook the apples as it is much nicer when the apples are just tender and retain their shape. Use a perforated spoon to remove apples to serving dish. Add the jam and sherry to the syrup remaining in the dish, microwave at HIGH 8 or 9 minutes, stirring once, and cook until syrup has a nice texture. Pour over the apples. Cool and refrigerate until ready to serve.

Honey Bee Apples

Do not let the simplicity of this dessert stop you from making it, even when an elegant dessert is your wish.

6 baking apples	**1/2 tsp. (2 mL) nutmeg**
2/3 cup (160 mL) honey	**2 tbsp. (30 mL) rum**
The grated rind of 1 orange	**Juice of 1/2 an orange**

Core the apples, and starting at the stem end, pare them one-third of the way down. Place them in a 2 x 8-inch (5 x 20 cm) baking dish. Fill each cavity with the honey, orange rind and nutmeg mixed together. Pour the rum mixed with the orange juice on top of the apples. Microwave 6 minutes at HIGH. Baste apples with the juice in the bottom of the dish. Microwave at MEDIUM 4 to 5 minutes, or until the apples are tender. Serve hot or cold.

Apple Allegro

There are two pleasant ways to serve these apples: warm, with whipped cream on top or over ice cream, cold, as they are on top of sponge cake.

6 medium apples, peeled	**4 tbsp. (60 mL) brown sugar**
2 tbsp. melted butter	**2 tsp. (10 mL) brandy**
Lemon juice	**1/2 tsp. (2 mL) cinnamon**

Cut the peeled apples into quarters, core. Arrange in a single layer, core-side down, in a buttered baking dish.
Brush with melted butter. Sprinkle with lemon juice to taste, brown sugar, brandy and cinnamon, microwave 10 minutes at HIGH.
Baste several times with the juice in the bottom of the dish. Serve as you wish.

Caramel Apples

Quick and easy, I like to make these all year round, but especially when the first Melba apples are around. These apples have a very short season and are not good keepers, but they are worth looking for.

1/3 cup (80 mL) butter or margarine

1 cup (250 mL) brown sugar

1/2 tsp. (2 mL) cinnamon or allspice

4 to 6 apples, peeled, cored and cut in four

1 tsp. (5 mL) vanilla extract

2 tbsp. (30 mL) cream

Place the butter or margarine in a 9-inch (22.5 cm) pie plate. Microwave at HIGH 2 minutes. Stir in the brown sugar and the spice of your choice until well mixed. Place the apples over this sugar mixture. Microwave 6 to 7 minutes at HIGH, the time depending on the variety of apples used — they should be soft when touched with the point of a knife, but not mushy. Remove the cooked apples to a serving dish.

Add the cream and vanilla extract to the syrup in the plate. Microwave 3 to 5 minutes at HIGH, stirring twice. When the syrup has thickened, pour over the apples. Let stand about 1 hour at room temperature before serving.

If you wish to make these early in the day, simply warm them up 1 minute at HIGH when ready to serve.

Poached Apples

I make these when apples are past their prime (middle or end of winter). Quick and easy to prepare and most tasty.

5 to 6 apples, peeled and cut in four

1/2 cup (125 mL) brown sugar

1/2 cup (125 mL) water or apple juice

Grated rind and juice of 1/2 a lemon or orange

2 tbsp. (30 mL) jam of your choice

2 tbsp. (30 mL) sherry (optional)

Place in a bowl the brown sugar, water or apple juice, the lemon or orange grated rind and juice. Microwave at HIGH 3 minutes. Stir well, add the apples, stir and microwave at HIGH 5 to 7 minutes, stirring once during the cooking period. Place the apples on a serving dish, draining as much syrup as possible. Add the remaining ingredients to the syrup. Stir. Microwave at HIGH 1 minute, pour over the apples. Cool, cover and refrigerate until ready to serve.

Maple Poached Apples

This is a truly Canadian recipe. Maple syrup and apples are usually on hand in most households.

4 to 5 apples

1/3 cup (80 mL) maple syrup

3 tbsp. (50 mL) butter

A pinch of allspice (optional)

Place in a 9-inch (22.5 cm) pie plate (ceramic or Pyrex), the maple syrup, butter and allspice. Microwave 2 minutes at HIGH. Peel and core apples, cut in four. Roll in the hot syrup. Microwave 3 minutes at HIGH. Turn the apple quarters. Microwave 4 to 5 minutes at HIGH.
Serve hot or cold, but do not refrigerate.

Pink or Purple Applesauce (photo opposite p. 33, top right)

One day I had a cup of cranberries in my freezer that somehow never seemed to be used. I took them out, and as I had 6 apples in my fruit basket, I thought why not try cooking them together in the microwave oven. That was three years ago, and I still enjoy this applesauce.

6 apples, peeled, cored and sliced

1 cup (250 mL) uncooked cranberries

1 cup (250 mL) sugar

1 tbsp. (15 mL) fresh lemon juice

Freshly grated nutmeg, to taste*

Place in a 4-cup (1 L) dish, the apples, cranberries, sugar and lemon juice. Microwave at HIGH 10 minutes. Stir well and microwave 2 to 3 minutes at MEDIUM. Stir again, pour into serving dish. Top with the grated nutmeg.

* *It is much more economical to buy whole nutmeg and a nutmeg grater — and grate whatever you require, then put nutmeg away. It will keep fragrant, whole, for 2 to 3 years.*

Helpful Hint

To roast nuts, place 1/4 cup (60 mL) nuts in a glass pie plate. Microwave 3 to 4 minutes at HIGH, stirring twice.

Apple Crisp

Depending on the occasion, I like to serve this apple crisp hot topped with very cold ice cream, or cold with a creamy butterscotch sauce (see index), or with a small decanter of hot rum for each one to use to taste.

4 cups (1 L) apples, peeled and sliced

1/3 cup (80 mL) sugar

2 tbsp. (30 mL) flour

1/2 tsp. (2 mL) cinnamon or
   1/4 tsp. (1 mL) ground cardamom

1 tbsp. (15 mL) margarine or butter

2 tbsp. (30 mL) lemon juice

Topping

3/4 cup (190 mL) brown sugar

3/4 cup (190 mL) flour

1/3 cup (80 mL) butter

2 tbsp. (30 mL) chopped nuts

A pinch of salt

A pinch of cinnamon or cardamom

Slice apples into an 8 x 8-inch (20 x 20 cm) microwave-safe dish. Mix together the sugar, flour, cinnamon or cardamom and margarine or butter and sprinkle over the apples. Pour lemon juice over all. Mix the topping ingredients together. Sprinkle over the apples, press down all over with a knife. Microwave 10 minutes at HIGH, and 8 or 9 minute at MEDIUM-HIGH, until the topping is cooked and lightly browned.

English Galette

An old-fashioned English luncheon dessert served with a bowl of cinnamon sugar, prepared with 1 teaspoon (5 mL) cinnamon and 1 cup (250 mL) sugar.

1½ cups (375 mL) milk

2 eggs, beaten

1½ cups (375 mL) flour

2 tsp. (10 mL) baking powder

2 tbsp. (30 mL) sugar

1/2 tsp. (2 mL) salt

2 tbsp. (30 mL) butter

4 medium apples, peeled, cored and coarsely
   grated or chopped

Juice and grated rind of 1 lemon

Add beaten eggs to milk, beat a few seconds. Mix together the flour, baking powder, sugar and salt. Add to milk mixture, stir. Place the butter in a small bowl and microwave 40 seconds at HIGH. Stir the melted butter into the mixture.
Mix together the grated or chopped apples, the lemon juice and rind. Add to batter, mix well and place in a round 10½-inch (26 cm) microwave-safe dish. Microwave at HIGH 10 minutes. There may be an inch round spot in the middle that is still soft. If so, microwave another 2 minutes at HIGH.
Sprinkle top with a spoonful or two or dark brown sugar, let stand 10 minutes.

Baked Rhubarb

You may become addicted to this just as I am. I sometimes use 10 to 12 wild rose petals chopped fine with rose water or chopped fresh wild roses (2 or 3 will be sufficient for the following recipe).

2 cups (500 mL) rhubarb

2 tbsp. (30 mL) water

A pinch of salt

1/2 cup (125 mL) sugar

1/8 tsp. (.05 mL) rose water*

Clean and cut the rhubarb in 1/2-inch (1 cm) pieces. Place in an 8-cup (2 L) microwave-safe dish, add water and salt.
Microwave 4 minutes at HIGH, stirring once. Add sugar, rose water or chopped wild roses. Let stand 3 minutes. Stir thoroughly.
Variation: Sugar may be replaced by an equal quantity of honey. Sprinkle top with grated rind of 1 orange and a dash of nutmeg.

* Rose water is sold in drug stores or at Speciality Food Shops.

Rhubarb and Strawberry Compote

An old classic dessert in France, in England, in Italy and surely in Canada. I consider it an annual must.

4 cups (1 L) fresh rhubarb, cleaned and diced

1/2 cup (125 mL) fresh orange juice

1 cup (250 mL) sugar

2 cups (500 mL) fresh strawberries, cleaned and cut in two

Clean and cut the fresh rhubarb into 1/2-inch (1 cm) pieces. Place in an 8-cup (2 L) dish, add the orange juice and the sugar. Stir and microwave at HIGH 4 to 5 minutes, stirring twice. When the rhubarb is cooked and hot, add the strawberries, stir gently. Cover with a plate or a paper. Let stand 2 to 3 hours at room temperature. Serve as is or with cream or over ice cream. I prefer it served with a bowl of commercial sour cream.

Helpful Hint

To remove brown skin from almonds, place almonds in a bowl, cover with water, microwave 5 minutes at HIGH per cup. Cool and rub between your fingers to remove skins.

Rhubarb Crisp

An old Canadian favorite. To my family, spring appears only when I make Rhubarb Crisp with fresh cut rhubarb from the garden.

2 cups (500 mL) rhubarb

2 tbsp. (30 mL) lemon juice

1/2 cup (125 mL) sugar

Grated rind of 1/2 a lemon

1 cup (250 mL) brown sugar

3/4 cup (190 mL) flour

1/4 cup (60 mL) rolled oats

1/2 cup (125 mL) soft butter

Wash and cut rhubarb into 1/2-inch (1 cm) pieces. Add lemon juice and sugar. Mix well. Place in an 8 x 8-inch (20 x 20 cm) baking dish, sprinkle lemon rind on top. Mix together brown sugar, flour, rolled oats and butter until crumbly. Sprinkle on top of the rhubarb. Microwave 10 minutes at HIGH and 5 minutes at MEDIUM. Serve hot or at room temperature.

Jellied Rhubarb

In the winter when only frozen rhubarb is available, I enjoy making this fast, easy and tasty dessert.

1 lb (500 g) frozen rhubarb*

1/3 cup (80 mL) water

1 package (175 mL) strawberry or peach Jell-O or other jelly powder

Place in a bowl the frozen rhubarb and the water. Microwave at HIGH 8 to 9 minutes, stirring well after 5 minutes of cooking. Place the Jell-O or other jelly powder in a serving dish, pour the hot rhubarb over and stir until thoroughly mixed, the heat of the rhubarb is sufficient to dissolve the granulated gelatine. Refrigerate until ready to serve as is or topped with cream, whipped cream or ice cream.

* The frozen rhubarb I like best is sold in 1 kg bags. Half the bag is used to make this dessert.

Strawberry Compote

The strawberries will not cook in the 40 seconds but they will absorb the warm syrup very quickly and become very tasty.

About 4 cups (1 L) fresh strawberries

1/4 to 1/2 cup (60 to 125 mL) honey

Grated rind and juice of 1/2 an orange

Wash and hull the strawberries, place in a bowl and microwave 40 seconds at HIGH. Place the honey over the berries, add the grated orange rind and juice, microwave 1 minute at HIGH. Stir gently, cover and refrigerate 3 to 4 hours.

Jiffy Strawberry Compote

A simple, easy dessert with a delectable flavor. I like to serve it with small meringue cookies.

3 to 4 cups (750 mL to 1 L) fresh strawberries

1/2 cup (125 mL) fruit sugar

The grated rind of 1 orange

The juice of 1/2 an orange

1 tbsp. (15 mL) orange liqueur or sherry (optional)

Mix all the ingredients together. Place in a microwave-safe serving dish. Microwave 2 minutes at MEDIUM-LOW. Stir gently, by shaking the bowl, rather than by stirring with a spoon. Keep at room temperature until ready to serve.

Strawberry Pudding
(Convection)

The famous English Summer Pudding, which is made with raspberries and served cold, was the inspiration for this.* I prefer to serve it tepid, as the fruit flavor is more pronounced.

4 cups (1 L) strawberries

Juice of 1/2 a lemon

2/3 cup (160 mL) brown sugar

4 cups (1 L) toasted bread cubes

1/4 cup (60 mL) white sugar

Grated rind of 1 lemon

2 tbsp. (30 mL) butter

Wash and hull the berries and mix them with the lemon juice and brown sugar. Place mixture in a shallow 6-cup (1.5 L) pan. Mix the bread cubes, white sugar and lemon rind. Sprinkle over the strawberries, but do not mix.
Dot with butter, place on rack and bake 25 to 30 minutes in the convection part of the microwave oven preheated to 350°F. (180°C) for 15 minutes. Serve warm or tepid with cold, rich or sour cream.

* See index.

Strawberries with cream

A hot syrup poured over fresh strawberries, then refrigerated to chill is a "gourmet" experience. Do try them when in full season. I like to serve them with sweetened whipped cream or plain cream, flavored with a few drops of rose water.*

1/4 cup (60 mL) water or apple juice

1/4 cup (60 mL) sugar

2 tbsp. (30 mL) of a liqueur of your choice (optional)

4 to 6 cups (1 to 1.5 L) fresh strawberries

Place the sugar, water or apple juice in a measuring cup. Microwave 2 minutes at MEDIUM-HIGH, stirring once. Add to the hot syrup the liqueur of your choice, a few drops of rose water, if you wish, or omit the liqueur and use only the rose water. Mix well and pour the hot syrup over the strawberries. Stir gently, preferably with your hands. Cover and refrigerate until ready to serve.

* Rose water may be purchased at certain drugstores or at Speciality Food Shops.

French Strawberry Mousse

This dessert is super and a favorite in many countries, Italy, France, Germany, Switzerland, to name but a few. Each one has variations to their taste. So, try it and find out if you would prefer your own variation. Mine is the addition of a teaspoon (5 mL) of rose water or half a cup of wild roses (they must be the wild type), chopped, or I add a small handful that I microwave 3 minutes at HIGH, stirring once. Make it once and take it from there to choose your own creation.

4 cups (1 L) fresh strawberries	1 cup (250 mL) whipping cream
1 cup (250 mL) fruit sugar	1 tsp. (5 mL) vanilla extract
2 tbsp. (30 mL) fresh lemon juice	2 envelopes unflavored gelatine
2 egg whites	3/4 cup (190 mL) cold water

Clean and slice the strawberries, place in a bowl with the fruit sugar and lemon juice. Stir gently and set aside.

Beat the egg whites until stiff and whip the cream, add the vanilla, mix.

Place the unflavored gelatine in a measuring cup, add the cold water. Microwave 2 to 3 minutes at MEDIUM. It is ready when all the gelatine is dissolved, stir well and let cool slightly. Now that all is ready, you must work fast. Pour the gelatine over the strawberries and stir thoroughly. Blend in the beaten egg whites, folding them gently into the mixture, then fold in the whipped cream. Pour into an attractive cut glass dish. Cover and refrigerate until ready to serve. To taste, you may top the **mousse** with whole strawberries and sprinkle them lightly with fruit sugar.

Strawberries Romanoff

A super classic dessert quickly and easily done in a microwave oven, without losing any of the delicate flavor of the fresh strawberries.

3 to 4 cups (750 mL to 1 L) fresh strawberries	1 cup (250 mL) whipping cream
1/2 cup (125 mL) fruit sugar	2 cups (500 mL) strawberry ice cream
1/4 tsp. (1 mL) rose water or 1/2 tsp. (2 mL) vanilla extract	2 tbsp. (30 mL) brandy or rum

Wash the strawberries quickly under running cold water (use a colander). Shake well, spread on a cloth to dry, about 30 minutes. Then, place in a bowl with the fruit sugar. Shake the bowl to distribute the sugar on the strawberries. Microwave 1 minute at MEDIUM. Shake the bowl gently and microwave another minute at MEDIUM-LOW. Refrigerate 1 hour.

Whip the cream (do not sweeten) and refrigerate, it can be refrigerated as long as the strawberries. When ready to serve, remove the ice cream from the freezer, uncover and microwave 1 minute at MEDIUM-HIGH to soften. Place in a bowl, add the whipped cream and the brandy or the rum. Mix well and fold in the strawberries. Serve as soon as ready.

Mrs. Cooke's Strawberry Swirl

I found this recipe in a Nova Scotia cookbook entitled "The Mixing Bowl", I adapted it to the microwave and made it many times, always with the same pleasure.

Crust:
1/4 cup (60 mL) butter

1 cup (250 mL) crushed graham wafers
1 tbsp. (15 mL) sugar

In an 8 x 8-inch (20 x 20 cm) ceramic dish or pie plate, melt the butter 2 minutes at HIGH. Add the graham crackers and the sugar, mix well. Remove 1/3 cup (80 mL) and reserve as topping. Spread the remaining crumbs all over the dish or pie plate to make a crust.
Place in a 4-cup (1 L) measuring cup:

1/2 cup (125 mL) milk
1/2 lb (250 g) marshmallows

Microwave 3 minutes at MEDIUM. Stir well, to make sure all the marshmallows have melted. Cool. Whip 1 cup (250 mL) cream, fold into the cooled mixture. Mix well and pour over graham cracker crust.

Topping :
1 package strawberry Jell-O or other brand
  of jelly powder
1 cup (250 mL) boiling water

1 cup (250 mL) cold apple juice or cold water
2 cups (500 mL) fresh sliced strawberries or
  1 box (245 g) thawed out sliced strawberries

Mix the Jell-O or other jelly powder with the boiling water until well dissolved, add the apple juice or cold water. Refrigerate until barely set. Fold in the strawberries.
Pour over the marshmallow filling already in the pie. Sprinkle remaining crumb mixture on top. Refrigerate 2 to 4 hours before serving.

Summer Pudding

An English classic, to be made when fresh raspberries are in season.

2 cups (500 mL) fresh raspberries
1/2 cup (125 mL) sugar
1 tsp. (5 mL) lemon juice

6 thin slices white bread, buttered
Whipped cream

Place the cleaned raspberries in a microwave-safe dish, add the sugar. Microwave 6 minutes at HIGH, stirring twice. Add lemon juice, stir well. Do not strain.
Place a few slices of buttered bread in the bottom of a serving dish. Cover with as much of the raspberry syrup as the bread will absorb. Repeat procedure until all is used.
Cover and refrigerate 6 to 8 hours. Unmold or serve from dish with whipped cream.

Blueberry Dumplings (p. 35) →

English Raspberry Pudding

A true English pudding almost as old as England. It has gone through many transformations. Here is another one since I adapted it to microwave cooking. To me, this pudding is a must when raspberries are at their peak, end of June or early July.

4 cups (1 L) raspberries	**1/4 cup (60 mL) white sugar**
Juice of 1/2 a lemon	**Grated rind of 1 small lemon**
2/3 cup (160 mL) light brown sugar	**2 tbsp. (30 mL) butter**
4 cups (1 L) toasted bread cubes	

Wash and hull the berries, mix them with the lemon juice and brown sugar. Pour into an 8 x 8-inch (20 x 20 cm) baking dish. (I like to use a Corning ceramic dish for this pudding).
Mix the bread cubes, white sugar and grated lemon rind. Spread over the raspberries. Press mixture gently together, but do not stir. Dot all over with the butter. Microwave 4 minutes at HIGH. Serve hot or cool, but not refrigerated. Serve as is or top with ice cream or cream.

Fresh Raspberry Bavarian Cream (photo opposite bottom right)

A cool, creamy summer delight. I never miss making this cream when the fresh raspberries are with us.

1 cup (250 mL) water	**1 banana, sliced (optional)**
1 package (3 oz - 74 g) raspberry flavored gelatine	**1 cup (250 mL) mashed fresh raspberries**
2 cups (500 mL) vanilla ice cream	

Place water in a 4-cup (1 L) measure. Microwave at HIGH 2 minutes, or until it boils. Stir in the gelatine until dissolved. Add ice cream, stir until melted. Stir in the mashed fruit. Pour into a nice glass dish. Refrigerate 3 to 6 hours. Unmold on a large plate, surround with more sweetened berries.

← Left: Pears Florentine (p. 36) and Zabaglione (p. 22)
← Top right: Pink or Purple Applesauce (p. 26)
← Center right: Rum Grapefruit (p. 44)
← Bottom right: Fresh Raspberry Bavarian Cream (recipe above)

Sauce Parisienne

Try to use vanilla bean* to make this sauce, or replace by a teaspoon (5 mL) of vanilla extract, that you add after the creamy custard is cooked.

1/2 cup (125 mL) milk

1/2 cup (125 mL) whipping cream

2 inches (5 cm) of vanilla bean*

2 egg yolks

1/4 cup (60 mL) sugar

1 cup (250 mL) fresh raspberries

1 cup (250 mL) whipping cream

Place in a bowl, the milk, whipping cream and vanilla bean (if you do use it). Microwave 2 minutes at HIGH.
Beat the egg yolks with the sugar and add to the hot milk. Stir until well mixed. Microwave 5 minutes at MEDIUM, stirring twice. It is sometimes necessary to microwave one minute more at MEDIUM.
Remove the vanilla bean. At this point, add the liquid vanilla if you have not used the vanilla bean.
Wash the raspberries and pass through a strainer to make a purée, or simply add them to the sauce.
Whip the cream and fold into the sauce. Serve at room temperature or warm.

* You can buy vanilla beans at good speciality shops. Keep in a box of fruit sugar. You can use as much as 2 cups (500 mL) of fruit sugar, even with only 1 vanilla bean; the whole sugar will take the vanilla flavor. Use with fresh fruit or in any sauce you wish to flavor with vanilla. When you have used the vanilla stick in a liquid, as you do in this recipe, let it dry 6 to 8 hours on a paper towel and put it back in the sugar. Keep it well buried in the sugar.

How to make vanilla extract

Once you try this you will always make it. . . the word superlative is not too much for it.

1 bottle (341 mL) Bacardi rum (40% alc.)

3 vanilla beans

Add vanilla to rum. Shake well. Let ripen 3 to 4 weeks in a dark cupboard. Use in the same quantity as ordinary vanilla extract, according to your recipe. When the bottle of rum is half full, simply fill with more rum and add another vanilla bean. When a recipe calls for a vanilla bean, simply take it out of the rum and add to your recipe, remove it when ready, wash it and put it back into the rum.
Vanilla made this way is far more economical than buying vanilla extract and many times more tasty.

Blueberry Dumplings

At least once a year treat! Super served hot with vanilla ice cream.

Sauce:
2½ cups (625 mL) fresh blueberries
1/3 cup (80 mL) sugar
A good pinch of salt
1 cup (250 mL) water
1 tbsp. (15 mL) fresh lemon juice

Dumplings:
1 cup (250 mL) all-purpose flour
2 tbsp. (30 mL) sugar
2 tsp. (10 mL) baking powder
1/4 tsp. (1 mL) salt
1 tbsp. (15 mL) butter
1/2 cup (125 mL) milk

Place in a 4-cup (1 L) bowl, the blueberries, sugar, salt, water and lemon juice. Microwave 4 minutes at HIGH. Stir well. Sift together in a bowl, the flour, sugar, baking powder and salt. Cut in the butter with a knife. Add the milk, all at once, stir only until flour is dampened.
Microwave the above blueberry sauce 3 minutes at HIGH. Drop batter in the hot blueberries from the tip of a tablespoon (15 mL). You should have 6 to 7 dumplings.
Cover and microwave 6 minutes at HIGH. Serve as is or with cream or ice cream.

Berry Crisp

Serve hot or tepid, with cream or whipped cream or yogurt, to taste. In the summer, I use fresh berries. In the winter, I replace them with frozen fruit.

3 cups (750 mL) fresh strawberries, raspberries
  or blueberries or 1 package (15 oz - 425 mL)
  frozen berries of your choice
2 tbsp. (30 mL) lemon juice
2/3 cup (160 mL) brown sugar
1/2 cup (125 mL) flour

2/3 cup (160 mL) rolled oats
1/3 cup (80 mL) margarine or butter
3/4 tsp. (3 mL) cinnamon
1/4 tsp. (1 mL) allspice
1/4 tsp. (1 mL) salt

Place the berries in a microwave-safe baking dish 8 x 8-inch (20 x 20 cm). Pour the lemon juice on top. Mix the remaining ingredients, sprinkle over the fruit. Microwave 7 to 8 minutes at HIGH. Let stand 15 minutes before serving.

Pears Melba

A colorful and delicious dessert of fresh pears when you are looking for a buffet dessert.

A 10-oz (300 g) package frozen raspberries	2 tbsp. (30 mL) lemon juice
1/2 cup (125 mL) sugar	1 tbsp. (15 mL) brandy (optional)
1 tbsp. (15 mL) cornstarch	4 to 6 pears, peeled

Place the frozen raspberries in a 4-cup (1 L) dish. Microwave uncovered at HIGH 3 minutes, turn over and microwave 2 to 3 minutes more.
Blend together the sugar, cornstarch, lemon juice and brandy. Microwave 2 minutes at MEDIUM-HIGH. Add raspberries and stir.
Pour over the peeled pears cut in halves. Microwave covered at HIGH 5 to 9 minutes, depending on size and ripeness of pears. Check for doneness, and if necessary microwave 2 or 3 minutes more at HIGH. Serve warm or cold, as is or topped with whipped cream or ice cream.

Note: This recipe was developed with Bosc winter pears, the very best pears to poach or microwave.

Pears Florentine (photo opposite p. 33, left)

Another quick and delectable Italian dessert that can be served hot or at room temperature.

1/3 cup (80 mL) slivered almonds	1/2 cup (125 mL) sugar
1 tbsp. (15 mL) butter	1/4 tsp. (1 mL) almond extract
4 to 6 pears, peeled, halved and cored	1/2 cup (125 mL) white wine or vermouth

Place the almonds and the butter in a saucer, microwave about 2 minutes at HIGH, stirring once or twice. They should be browned lightly. If the almonds are very cold (I keep mine frozen), they may take a minute more to brown. However, that is easy to judge.
Place the pears in a ceramic pie plate, core side up, the large part on the rim of the plate. Stir together the sugar, toasted almonds and the almond extract, fill the cavity of each pear with some of this almond sugar.
Pour the wine into the bottom of the plate. Microwave 6 minutes at HIGH. Serve at room temperature. For a spectacular dessert, serve with a Zabaglione (see index) as a sauce.

Wine Poached Pears

Whenever I have leftover white wine or Sake, plus fresh pears, I make these delicious pears and serve them hot or at room temperature. In the winter, I defrost a cup or two of my unsweetened berries to which I add about 1/3 cup (80 mL) of sugar, I mash them and serve them as a sauce to accompany the poached pears.

4 to 5 pears, peeled, halved and cored

1 cup (250 mL) white wine or Sake

1/2 cup (125 mL) apple juice or soda water*

1/3 to 1/2 cup (80 to 125 mL) sugar

Place in a bowl all the ingredients except the pears. Stir and microwave 3 to 4 minutes at HIGH. Place the prepared pears in the syrup core-side down. Baste with the hot syrup. Microwave about 5 minutes at MEDIUM-HIGH. Baste the fruits with the syrup. Microwave another minute at MEDIUM-HIGH. Serve hot or cold.

* Soda water may be replaced by Seven-Up, ginger ale or tonic.

Pears in Lemon Cream

A very elegant and tasty way to serve pears. They may be served simply poached and kept in their syrup, or topped with the lemon cream. Another variation is to replace the lemon with 4 to 6 slices of lime.

1 cup (250 mL) water or apple juice

1/2 cup (125 mL) sugar

6 slices unpeeled lemon or lime

6 pears, peeled and cut in half

Lemon Custard

1/4 cup (60 mL) sugar

1 tbsp. (15 mL) cornstarch

1 cup (250 mL) light cream or milk

2 egg yolks

Place in a round 8 or 9-inch (20 or 22.5 cm) ceramic dish, the water or apple juice, sugar, slices of lemon or lime. Stir to mix. Microwave 10 minutes at HIGH. Stir well, place the peeled pears, halved and cored, in the hot syrup, with the small end toward the middle of the dish. Baste pears with the hot syrup. Microwave 4 to 5 minutes at HIGH, or until pears are tender. Test with the point of a knife. Baste once after 3 minutes of cooking.
Remove pears to a serving dish with a slotted spoon. Mix together the 1/4 cup (60 mL) sugar, the cornstarch and cream or milk, add the egg yolks. Mix thoroughly. Add mixture to the hot pear syrup. Stir well, microwave 1 minute at MEDIUM, stir well, microwave another 2 minutes, stirring once. The sauce should have a light, creamy texture. Pour hot over the pears. Cover and let stand until cooled, but do not refrigerate.

Pears "Glacées"

A famous recipe from the "répertoire" of the French chefs. Easy to prepare, glaze with apricot jam when ready to serve.

1 cup (250 mL) sugar

1 cup (250 mL) water

The rind of 1 orange

6 whole fresh pears, peeled

Vanilla or strawberry ice cream (optional)

1/2 cup (125 mL) apricot or strawberry jam

2 tbsp. (30 mL) liqueur of your choice

Place in a dish, the sugar, water and orange rind. Microwave 10 minutes at MEDIUM-HIGH.
Peel the pears, cut in half, remove core and place in the hot syrup, basting them 8 to 10 times, so the pears will be covered with the syrup. Microwave 6 to 8 minutes at HIGH. The pears should be tender, but not too soft.
Remove pears from the syrup*. Place on a serving dish.
Warm up the apricot or strawberry jam with the liqueur 40 seconds at HIGH. Brush each pear with this jam glaze. Add about 1/2 cup (125 mL) of the hot syrup in the bottom of the dish. Serve cold.

*Keep the remaining syrup in a glass jar, refrigerate. It can be used to poach any fruit. It will keep 5 to 6 months.

Helpful Hint

To soften hardened brown sugar, place in a dish with a slice of fresh bread or a quarter of an apple, cover and microwave 15 to 40 seconds at HIGH (for 1 cup (250 mL).

Fruit Cobbler

This microwaved fruit cobbler can be served simply as fruit cooked in a syrup, using a single type of fruit or a mixture of your choice, or topped with the batter it then becomes a cobbler pudding.

1/3 cup (80 mL) sugar

1 tbsp. (15 mL) cold water

2 cups (500 mL) fresh fruit, peeled (plums, peaches, apples or pears, etc.)

1 tbsp. (15 mL) cornstarch

1/2 tsp. (2 mL) vanilla or almond extract

Topping batter

1 cup (250 mL) all-purpose flour

1 tsp. (5 mL) baking powder

1/2 tsp. (2 mL) salt

2 tbsp. (30 mL) brown sugar

1/2 cup (125 mL) milk

1 egg

1 tbsp. (15 mL) soft butter or margarine

2 tsp. (10 mL) brown sugar

1/4 tsp. (1 mL) cinnamon

Place in a dish of your choice the sugar and water. Microwave 2 minutes at HIGH. Add 1 cup (250 mL) of the peeled fruit left whole, or sliced or cut in four. Stir the cornstarch into this mixture, mix well and microwave 2 minutes at HIGH, stirring every minute. Some fruits may require an extra minute.
The syrup which thickens almost instantly forms a glaze over the fruit, which is why it is important to stir well every minute. When the sauce is creamy and transparent, add the remaining cup of fruit and the vanilla or almond extract. Microwave 1 minute at HIGH.
Serve as is for a fruit dessert, or place in an 8-inch (20 cm) round baking dish to make a Cobbler.
Cobbler dough: Sift together the flour, baking powder and salt. Stir in the brown sugar. Beat the egg and the milk together. Add to mixture with the soft butter or margarine and stir. When dough forms a soft ball, drop dough by spoonfuls on top of the hot fruit compote (if fruit has cooled, microwave 1 minute at HIGH).
Mix the brown sugar and cinnamon, sprinkle over dough, cover with waxed paper and microwave 4 to 5 minutes at MEDIUM-HIGH, turning casserole a quarter turn halfway through cooking period if your oven does not have a turntable.

Helpful Hint

To melt chocolate, place one square of chocolate in a dish. Microwave 2 to 3 minutes at MEDIUM-LOW. Check before adding more time.

Fresh Peaches "à l'Anglaise"

Use your microwave oven to peel the peaches in no time, with the greatest of ease. Place the peaches (6 to 8) in a circle and microwave 15 seconds at HIGH. Let them stand 10 minutes on the counter and peel.

4 to 6 peaches	1/4 cup (60 mL) slivered almonds
1 tbsp. (15 mL) fresh lemon juice	2 pinches of nutmeg
2 tbsp. (30 mL) sugar	2 tbsp. (30 mL) brandy*

Peel peaches, cut in half and remove pits. Coat lightly with lemon juice.
Place peaches in an 8 x 8-inch (20 x 20 cm) microwave-safe baking dish, open side up, sprinkle with the sugar.
Mix together the almonds and nutmeg in a pie plate, microwave uncovered 3 minutes at HIGH, stirring once. Fill peach cavities with the almonds, microwave uncovered 5 minutes at HIGH. Pour brandy on top, let stand 5 minutes.

* I recommend using Mont Blanc White Brandy which is economical and very good for cooking.

Creamy Peaches

Another French delight, a super dessert where the peaches are barely cooked and the light pudding on top can be served at room temperature or refrigerated.

2 cups (500 mL) fresh peaches, peeled and sliced	1/4 cup (60 mL) flour
3 eggs	1 tsp. (5 mL) vanilla
1/2 cup (125 mL) sugar	1 cup (250 mL) light or heavy cream
1/2 tsp. (2 mL) ground nutmeg*	1/2 cup (125 mL) dry white wine or vermouth

Peel the fresh peaches and slice into an 8-inch (20 cm) baking dish (Corning or Pyrex).
Place the remaining ingredients in a bowl. Mix thoroughly with a rotary beater, pour over the peaches, microwave at MEDIUM-HIGH uncovered 6 to 8 minutes. Check doneness with the point of a knife, especially in the middle of the dish. If necessary, microwave 1 or 2 minutes longer.
When cold, top with about 1/4 cup (60 mL) jelly or jam of your choice melted 40 seconds at HIGH in the microwave.

Note: I strongly recommend the use of nutmeg bought whole and grated finely according to your needs (special nutmeg graters are found in kitchenware boutiques). It is readily available at spice counters, and will keep indefinitely. Whole nutmeg, freshly grated, is highly superior in flavor to ground nutmeg, and much more economical.

Portuguese Peaches

Madeira wine which gives them their personality, comes from Portugal. I always keep a bottle of it in my kitchen, as it is equally good in a gravy, especially with beef or lamb, and it is "super" in desserts.

4 to 5 fresh peaches

1/3 cup (80 mL) butter

2/3 cup (160 mL) sugar

1/3 cup (80 mL) Madeira wine

Peel peaches, remove stones and cut in half.
Melt the butter in a 9-inch (22.5 cm) pie plate 2 minutes at HIGH. The butter will brown lightly here and there, but that is as it should be. Stir in the sugar, microwave at HIGH 1 minute, stir and microwave another 1 to 2 minutes, or until sugar caramelizes. Add the Madeira wine, stir, microwave 1 minute at MEDIUM. Place peach halves in this syrup rounded side up. Baste 3 to 4 times with the syrup, then microwave at MEDIUM-HIGH 3 to 4 minutes, basting the peaches with the syrup after 2 minutes of cooking.
Remove peaches from the syrup. Microwave syrup 2 minutes at MEDIUM-HIGH. Pour over the peaches.
Serve cold, as is or over ice cream or topped with cream.
Make sure the dessert is well covered when placed in the refrigerator.

Deep Dish Peach Pie
(Convection)

I make this when fresh peaches are available. When the season is over, I use the good dependable apple, both are good. This pie is best when cooked in the convection part of the microwave oven.

6 to 8 fresh peaches

1 tbsp. (15 mL) lemon juice

1/4 cup (60 mL) flour

1 cup (250 mL) brown sugar

1/4 cup (60 mL) soft butter or margarine

1/2 tsp. (2 mL) almond extract

Pastry of your choice for a 9-inch pie crust

1 egg yolk, beaten

2 tsp. (10 mL) water

1 tsp. (5 mL) sugar

Peel and slice the peaches, sprinkle with the lemon juice. Toss together gently. Mix the flour, brown sugar and butter or margarine, melted 1 minute at HIGH. Add to the sliced peaches, stir, add the almond extract.
Place mixture in a 9-inch (22.5 cm) x 2½ inches (7 cm) deep dish. Top with the pastry of your choice. Brush the pastry with the egg yolk beaten with the water. Sprinkle the teaspoon (5 mL) of sugar on top. Preheat convection part of the microwave oven to 375°F. (190°C) 15 minutes. Place pie on rack and bake 45 minutes or until golden brown. Cool on rack. Serve warm or at room temperature, to taste with whipped or plain cream, yogurt, sour cream or ice cream.
Variation: When this deep dish pie is made with apples, peel and slice the apples. Replace the almond extract by vanilla extract or use lemon or orange rind. About 1/2 teaspoon (2 mL) ground cardamom or coriander may be added.

Poached Canned Peaches

They are poached in a creamy sauce which takes away the "canned feeling". I sometimes pour the hot peaches and their sauce over a light white cake, replacing the vanilla extract in the cake by an equal quantity of almond extract.

1/3 cup (80 mL) sugar

2 tbsp. (30 mL) cornstarch

Grated rind of an orange

1 can (14 oz - 398 mL or 26 oz - 796 mL) peach halves

1/4 cup (60 mL) white wine or sherry

Place in a bowl, the sugar, cornstarch and orange rind. Stir until well blended. Drain the peaches and add 1/3 cup (80 mL) of the syrup to the cornstarch mixture. Stir again until well mixed. Microwave 2 minutes at HIGH, stir well. Add the wine or sherry. Microwave at MEDIUM-HIGH 2 to 3 minutes, or until sauce is creamy and transparent. Add the peaches to the hot syrup. Stir until well mixed. Pour into the serving dish. Serve warm or cold. They can be refrigerated covered, with their flavor losing none of its quality.

Coated Fresh Fruit

A creamy orange flower water sauce poured hot over fresh uncooked fruit. Surprising and delectable.

2 tbsp. (30 mL) butter

2 tbsp. (30 mL) flour

1/2 cup (125 mL) cream

1/2 cup (125 mL) milk

1/2 cup (125 mL) vanilla or plain sugar

1 tsp. (5 mL) orange flower water*

3 cups (750 mL) fresh peeled and sliced fruit of your choice**

2 tbsp. (30 mL) vanilla or plain sugar

Melt the 2 tablespoons (30 mL) butter in a 4-cup (1 L) dish 1 minute at HIGH. Stir in the flour, add the cream, milk and sugar, stir to mix. Microwave 1 minute at HIGH, stir well, microwave 2 minutes at HIGH, stirring once, if necessary microwave another minute at HIGH, sauce should be creamy. Add orange flower water.

Peel and slice the fruit of your choice into a nice serving dish. If fresh fruit is not available, well drained canned fruit may be used, but will not be as delicate in flavor and texture. Sprinkle the fruit with the 2 tablespoons (30 mL) vanilla or plain sugar. A pleasant addition, when available, is chopped fresh mint leaves. Pour the hot sauce over the fruits. Do not mix, cover and refrigerate until cold.

 * Orange flower water may be purchased in speciality shops or drug stores.
 ** A mixture of fruit is more interesting, such as peaches, pears, oranges, especially when fresh. The canned fruit may be of one type.

Creole Bananas

Another one of my quick and easy desserts. In the summer I enjoy these Creole Bananas over ice cream.

3 tbsp. (50 mL) butter
1/3 cup (80 mL) brown sugar
2 tbsp. (30 mL) cream
1/4 tsp. (1 mL) cinnamon

1/4 tsp. (1 mL) nutmeg
4 to 5 bananas
1/4 cup (60 mL) rum

Melt the butter 1 minute at HIGH. Add the brown sugar, cream cinnamon and nutmeg. Mix thoroughly.
Slice the peeled bananas lengthwise and then on the width. Add to the brown sugar mixture. Stir well.
Microwave uncovered 3 minutes at HIGH, or until the syrup boils.
Add the rum and let stand 1 minute before serving.

Simone's Oriental Pumpkin

A dear friend from Egypt, who was an impulsive cook and created many fascinating dishes.

3 cups (750 mL) pumpkin
1/2 cup (125 mL) water
1/2 cup (125 mL) brown sugar
1/2 tsp. (2 mL) cinnamon

1/4 tsp. (1 mL) nutmeg
Grated rind and juice of 1 orange
Butter

Peel pieces of pumpkin and measure 3 cups (750 mL). Cut into thin half moons and place in an 8-inch (20 cm) dish, add the water. Microwave 5 minutes at HIGH, covered.
Sprinkle the pumpkin with the brown sugar mixed with the cinnamon and nutmeg. Sprinkle the orange juice and rind on top. Dot with butter.
Cover with waxed paper. Microwave 3 minutes at HIGH. Stir. Microwave 1 minute at HIGH. Serve hot or cold with cream or ice cream or as the Orientals do, topped with a 1-inch (2,5 cm) layer of crushed ice, which the guests remove as soon as served.

How to Peel and Section Citrus Fruits

Whether orange or grapefruit or lemon or lime, cut off all the rind and the **white skin** (as it is bitter). Easy to do if you use a fairly large **sharp** knife, and work around and around the fruit over a bowl to catch any of the juices.
To section the fruit whole, peel and cut down each wedge on both sides of each section, as close to the membrane as possible and push the section into the bowl. Of course, remove seeds if any.

Irish Sweet Oranges

A tasty dessert when in a hurry. Equally good hot or cold.

3 to 5 oranges

3 tbsp. (50 mL) orange marmalade

2 to 4 tbsp. (30 to 60 mL) whiskey or brandy

Slice the oranges into a bowl.
Place the marmalade and whiskey or brandy in a bowl, microwave 3 minutes at MEDIUM-HIGH. Stir and pour over the oranges. Refrigerate to cool completely or serve tepid.

Rum Grapefruit (photo opposite p. 33, center right)

Surprise your family and guests with hot grapefruit served as an entrée, or if you prefer use as a dessert. They can be prepared an hour or so in advance to be microwaved when ready to serve. The important point in this recipe is the fresh ginger as the powdered type will not be half as tasty.

1 large grapefruit

2 tsp. (10 mL) brown sugar

1 tsp. (5 mL) fresh ginger root, grated

1 tsp. (5 mL) butter

Rum (optional)

Cut grapefruit in half. Remove seeds if necessary. Cut around sections. Place each half on a serving dish. Sprinkle the brown sugar and ginger mixed together on top of each half. Dot with butter and pour a teaspoon (5 mL) of rum over each half, if you wish.
Prepare as many as you require in the same manner. Microwave uncovered 5 minutes at HIGH, 4 at a time, placing them in a circle. If you wish to serve them hot, they will remain hot for 8 to 10 minutes.

Poached Fresh Grapefruit or Orange

Simply poached in a plain syrup or a liqueur-flavored type. I like to serve mine in a cut glass dish, either at room temperature or refrigerate 6 to 12 hours.

6 oranges or
2 to 3 grapefruits (according to size)

3/4 cup (190 mL) sugar

1/2 cup (125 mL) water

Grand Marnier, brandy or a liqueur
of your choice

Using a potato peeler, cut the top thin rind from two oranges or 1 grapefruit. Be careful not to take any of the white skin. With a small, sharp knife, cut the rind into long, thin slivers. Place in a measuring cup, the sugar and water, add the orange or grapefruit rind. Stir well, microwave at HIGH 2 minutes, stirring once.
Peel and section the chosen fruit, place in a bowl. Pour over the hot syrup. Stir gently. Add the liqueur of your choice. Stir again, and pour over the fruit. Stir gently. Cover, refrigerate 4 to 12 hours. Remove from the refrigerator one hour before serving.

Cakes

General Knowledge on Cake Making

Like pies, cakes can be cooked by microwave in minutes, or cooked by the Convection Method of your microwave oven which will take the usual time. In both cases, I am sure you will enjoy the quality of the finished cakes.

Important Bits of Information
- The first thing to do, whatever recipe you are making, is to choose the pan your recipe requires, and to prepare it as required. To microwave, use Pyrex or Corning or plastic type such as Micro-Dur. To cook by convection, metal pans may be used, they are preferable for baking cakes.
- It is preferable for the texture of the baked cake to have all ingredients at room temperature, such as fat, flour, liquid, etc.
- Butter and margarine are the best fats to use in cake making, then come the vegetable fats such as Crisco, etc. Make sure either one is at room temperature.
- When your recipe calls for brown sugar, pale or dark, make sure the measuring cup is firmly packed.
- Perhaps the most important part of cake making is the creaming of the butter or other fat — before and after the addition of the sugar. The way I like to work this part is by beating the butter or other fat at room temperature, with a hand or electric beater until fat is fluffy and creamy. Then I add a few spoonfuls at a time of the measured sugar, beating until creamy, after each addition. Then I keep beating until I do not feel any grains of sugar, when tested between the tips of my fingers. This can take a little more time than just mixing, but it makes all the difference between a perfect light cake or **just a cake.**
- When the recipe calls for beaten egg whites to be folded into the batter, do not use an electric mixer, do it by hand. It takes a little longer to do but does a great deal for the quality of the finished cake.
- Whether a cake is baked by microwave or by convection method, it should always be placed on a rack to bake as well as to cool to allow air to circulate all around, which keeps it light and perfect.
- Beat egg whites only to the stiff, shiny stage. If beaten too long, they become granular.
- **Folding** is an important part of cake making. When the recipe states to "Fold the beaten egg whites into the batter" this is the way to proceed:
  Beat the egg whites, then fold in about one-third of the beaten whites into the cake batter, mixing thoroughly, even folding them with a wire whisk or an egg beater.
  Then with a rubber spatula place the remaining beaten whites on top of the cake mixture. Then cut the spatula down from the center to the bottom of the bowl, and run it all over the bottom of the bowl and against the edge of the bowl, rotating it as you work. Keep gently repeating this process until all the beaten whites have been folded in. This is a bit lengthy to explain but you will find it is easy as you follow the procedure.

How to on Cakes

How to beat and fold egg whites into batter

1. The eggs must be separated carefully, make sure that no yolk particles are mixed in with the whites.
2. A greater volume of beaten whites will be obtained when they have been standing at least one hour at room temperature, before beating.
3. **"Beat to Soft Peak"** means that when air is added to the egg whites, through the beating process, the whites first expand and become fluffy and sort of creamy or opaque. If the recipe calls for sugar to be added "to the soft peak beaten egg whites", this is the point at which it should be added gradually.

   "Beat to Medium Peak" then the mixture should form rounded, glossy peaks when the beater is lifted from the bowl. Egg whites at this stage hold their shape and they are stiff and dry.

   "Beat to Stiff Peaks" continuing beating after reaching the "Medium Peaks" stage will result in stiffer and larger peaks.

This stage is used for meringue, pie topping, frosting, etc.

Beating further than indicated in the above three stages will only result in a dry and somewhat useless meringue.

To make a meringue or just beat the egg whites to a specific stage, use either an electric mixer or a hand beater or a wire whisk, the results are always good.

Measure the fats like a Chef

This is truly the **only** accurate method for measuring butter or any type of fat. It is referred to as "Water Displacement". It is simple. First, check your needs in the following table:

For 3/4 cup (190 mL) butter or shortening use 1/4 cup (60 mL) cold water
For 2/3 cup (160 mL) butter or shortening use 1/3 cup (80 mL) cold water
For 1/2 cup (125 mL) butter or shortening use 1/2 cup (125 mL) cold water
For 1/3 cup (80 mL) butter or shortening use 2/3 cup (160 mL) cold water
For 1/4 cup (60 mL) butter or shortening use 3/4 cup (190 mL) cold water

Place the proper amount of cold water given in the above table for the amount of fat you have to measure, then add the fat until the water reaches the one-cup (250 mL) level.

On flour

When a recipe calls for sifted flour, measure the demanded amount from flour that is first sifted. This is important as the weight and texture of the flour is different when sifted.

1 cup (250 mL) all-purpose flour **unsifted** = 4¼ ounces
1 cup (250 mL) all-purpose flour sifted = 3⅞ ounces

Preparing the cake pan
Some recipes call for a special way to prepare the cake pan or it is simply greased or greased and floured. Here is the way to do it.
To grease the pan, it takes about 1 teaspoon (5 mL) of shortening which is the best fat to use, for an 8 or 9 or 10-inch (20 or 22.5 or 25 cm) pan; spreading it with fingers is better than with a paper as too much of the fat gets into the paper, and the greasing is not equally done.
To flour a cake pan. Dust a bit of flour in the bottom of the chosen pan and shake the pan until the flour is well distributed.
To line a pan with paper. Lay the bottom of the pan over waxed or white or brown unglazed paper, trace around the edge with a pencil and just cut a bit outside the pencil mark. It will then fit to perfection in the bottom of the pan. But before placing the paper in the pan, grease one side, place it greased side down in the lightly greased pan, then grease the top side.
Always cool cooked cake on a rack.
Remember when adapting a favorite recipe that most cakes can be at their best whether microwaved or cooked in the convection part of the microwave oven, but some cakes cannot be cooked successfully by the microwave method, for example, angel food, sponge cakes, etc., but of course they can be baked in the convection part of your microwave oven.
Read your recipe before starting the cake to make sure which type of cooking is required.
The upside down type of cake is really the most successful when done by microwave, as the top of the microwaved cake will always remain pale yellow or whitish.
With an upside down cake, when unmolded (very easy to do) the appearance is good.
For the plain cake, topping the batter in the mold with 2 to 3 spoonfuls of chopped nuts of your choice mixed with 3 tablespoons (50 mL) of brown sugar spread on top of the raw batter before cooking will give it a very nice appearance. You will find examples in the following cake recipes.

Homemade Cake Mix (photo opposite p. 49, top)

This old recipe is free of any preservatives, and yet it may be kept for two to three months on a shelf in your kitchen cupboard, as long as it is stored in a metal or plastic container, or in a glass jar with a wide opening, and tightly covered.
One recipe will give you thirteen cups of mix. If you care to figure it out, you will realize how economical it is compared to commercial mixes and what savings are yours.

12 cups (3 L) all-purpose flour	**2 tbsp. (30 mL) salt**
1/4 cup (60 mL) + 2 tbsp. (30 mL) baking powder	**1$\frac{1}{3}$ cups (330 mL) instant powdered milk**

Sift the measured flour, add the baking powder and the salt, sift a second time. Add the powdered milk and mix thoroughly. Place in a container with tight fitting lid.

Commercial Type Cake
To prepare the cake, add 3 tablespoons (50 mL) vegetable oil for each cup (250 mL) of the mix, use water instead of the milk required in the recipe, flavor to taste. Use standard measuring cups and spoons for perfect results.
When preparing a cake or other recipe with this mix, put it in the measuring cup with a spoon, do not sift it before use, and do not pack it in the cup.
If the recipe calls for eggs, remove them from the refrigerator 5 to 10 minutes before making the cake.
Make sure that the molds you have are microwave-safe, or use Pyrex or Corning dishes.
The ideal size is 8 inches (20 cm).
For perfect results when baking a cake in the microwave oven, it is sometimes necessary to place a small inverted Pyrex dish in the middle of the mold and to pour the dough all around it. Choose a ring mold as a special mold for microwave baking. Remember that special plastic molds for microwave cooking must not be used in a conventional oven.

"Stir and Bake" Cake

This replaces the commercial cake mix. It is quick, it can be stirred in the mold and microwaved in no time.

2/3 cup (160 mL) of the mix

1/2 cup (125 mL) sugar

2 tbsp. (30 mL) instant powdered milk

1/4 cup (60 mL) vegetable oil

1 egg

1/4 cup (60 mL) + 2 tbsp. (30 mL) water

1/2 tsp. (2 mL) vanilla

Place in a bowl the mix, the sugar and powdered milk. Mix together the oil, egg and water. Pour over the dry ingredients together with the vanilla. Beat together for 1 minute.
Pour into an 8-inch (20 cm) mold, microwave 4 to 5 minutes at HIGH. Let stand 4 minutes and unmold.

Variations:
To make cupcakes, use paper cups placed in small microwave-safe molds and fill to half with the dough. Microwave 1½ to 2 minutes at HIGH.
Chocolate: To the cake recipe, add 3 tablespoons (50 mL) cocoa with 1 tablespoon (15 mL) brown sugar and 1 tablespoon (15 mL) more vegetable oil.
Lemon or Orange: To the cake recipe, add either 2 tablespoons (30 mL) lemon or orange juice and the grated rind of 1/2 a lemon or 1/2 an orange. Omit the 2 tablespoons (30 mL) water from the recipe.
Spicy: To the cake recipe, substitute brown sugar for the white sugar, add 1/4 teaspoon (1 mL) allspice, cinnamon and nutmeg. To taste, add 1/4 cup (60 mL) chopped nuts.

Chocolate Brownies with cake mix

3/4 cup (190 mL) homemade cake mix

1 cup (250 mL) sugar

6 tbsp. (90 mL) cocoa

1/4 cup (60 mL) butter or margarine

1/4 cup (60 mL) vegetable oil

2 eggs

1/2 cup (125 mL) chopped nuts

1 tsp. (5 mL) vanilla

In a 4-cup (1 L) measure, stir together with a fork the basic mix, sugar and cocoa. Place the butter or margarine in a 6 x 10-inch (15 x 25 cm) Pyrex or Corning dish and microwave 40 seconds at HIGH. Pour over the dry ingredients in the measuring cup, the oil and the eggs while stirring with the fork. Add the nuts and vanilla.
Pour into the melted butter, mix together for a few minutes with the fork, smooth the top of the cake, microwave 6 minutes at HIGH, turning the dish once during the cooking if you do not have a turntable. When cooked, let stand for 20 minutes on a cake rack and cut into squares.
To taste, roll each square in icing sugar.
These brownies freeze very well. To thaw, place one square on a white paper towel and microwave 30 seconds at HIGH.

Lovers' Apple Cake (p. 54) →

A Perfect One-egg Cake

This is a very old recipe which I adapted to microwave cooking. If you make the cake without the garnish, you will have a plain butter cake to serve as is, or to top with sweetened fresh fruit, such as strawberries, raspberries or blueberries.

If you microwave the cake with the given garnish or any variation of your choice in the bottom of the pan, you will have an attractive and tasty upside down cake, when unmolded.

The batter:

1/2 cup (125 mL) butter or margarine or shortening

1 cup (250 mL) sugar

1 egg

1 tsp. (5 mL) almond or vanilla extract

1⅔ cups (410 mL) flour

2 tsp. (10 mL) baking powder

1/4 tsp. (1 mL) salt

1/2 cup (125 mL) milk

Walnut mixture:

3 tbsp. (50 mL) butter or margarine

1/2 cup (125 mL) pale brown sugar

2 tbsp. (30 mL) all-purpose flour

1/2 cup (125 mL) chopped walnuts

3 tbsp. (50 mL) water or brandy or white wine

Beat in a bowl the butter, margarine or shortening until creamy. Add the sugar, egg and vanilla or almond extract and beat together until light and fluffy.

Mix together with a spoon the flour, baking powder and salt. Beat alternately with the milk into the creamed mixture. When well blended, if you wish to make a plain cake, pour the batter into an 8 x 8-inch (20 x 20 cm) baking dish, place on a rack and microwave 6 minutes at "MEDIUM-HIGH", checking doneness after 4 minutes. When done, cool on rack.

To make an upside down cake: Cream together the 3 tablespoons (50 mL) butter or margarine, the brown sugar and the 2 tablespoons (30 mL) flour. Add the chopped walnuts and the water, brandy or white wine. Stir. Spread in the bottom of the baking dish, buttered generously. Spoon the cake batter over this walnut mixture. Place the baking dish on a rack, microwave 3 minutes at MEDIUM-HIGH, give the cake a quarter turn and bake another 3 minutes. Test doneness same as for an oven baked cake. The finished cake when microwaved will be creamy yellow on top, and when unmolded it will have an attractive nut caramel topping.

Variation
Blueberry mixture:

2 to 3 cups (500 to 750 mL) blueberries

1/2 cup (125 mL) sugar

Grated rind of 1/2 a lemon

1/4 tsp. (1 mL) ginger or cinnamon

Mix all the ingredients together in the bottom of the baking dish and spread evenly. Spoon the cake batter over this mixture and microwave as given in "To make an upside down cake".

← **Top: Homemade Cake Mix (p. 47)**
← **Center: Christmas Plum Pudding (p. 61)**
← **Bottom: Lemon Cake (p. 52)**

Hélène's Favorite Quick Quick Cake

(photo opposite p. 57, bottom)

Quick to make, quick to bake, with many variations. A must in your cake "répertoire". A big plus, canned fruit or fresh fruit will make it equally flavorful.

The Batter:

1½ cups (375 mL) flour

3 tsp. (15 mL) baking powder

1 cup (250 mL) sugar

2 eggs + enough milk to give 1 cup (250 mL) of liquid

To flavor: Add **one** of the following **to the flour:**

1/2 tsp. (2 mL) nutmeg or allspice

1 tsp. (5 mL) ground cardamom or cinnamon

Grated lemon or orange rind

OR

Add **one** of the following **to the milk:**

1 tsp. (5 mL) vanilla extract

1/2 tsp. (2 mL) almond extract or rose water

2 tsp. (10 mL) liqueur of your choice

The Garnish:

2 tbsp. (30 mL) butter

2/3 cup (160 mL) pale brown sugar

3 tbsp. (50 mL) white wine or liquid drained from canned fruits

Canned fruit of your choice (apricots, peaches, pineapple, etc.), drained*

To prepare the batter: Mix together in a bowl the flour, baking powder, sugar and one of the **dry** flavorings, such as nutmeg, if you wish.
Place the eggs in a 1-cup (250 mL) measure and fill with milk. Add the liquid flavoring, such as vanilla. Pour into the dry ingredients and beat thoroughly with an electric beater.
To make an upside down cake: Place a small custard cup, open side down, in the middle of an 8 x 8-inch (20 x 20 cm) cake pan. Add the 2 tablespoons (30 mL) butter and microwave 1 minute at HIGH. Sprinkle the brown sugar over the butter, add the white wine or liquid drained from the canned fruit. Stir. Top with the chosen fruit. Pour the batter over all.
Place the cake pan on a microwave-safe rack and microwave 5 minutes at HIGH. Check doneness and microwave 2 or 3 minutes more at MEDIUM. Remove from oven and let stand 15 minutes on rack. Remove custard cup so that the juice accumulated under it will spread into the garnish.
To serve, cut into portions with the fruit mixture or other chosen garnish on top, or pass a knife around the cake and unmold.

* *You may replace canned fruit with nuts and coconut to taste*
  Or
  with raisins (about 3 tablespoons [50 mL])
  Or
  with 2 or 3 cups (500 or 750 mL) fresh fruit, such as strawberries, raspberries, blueberries, etc., sprinkled with 1/2 to 3/4 cup (125 to 190 mL) white sugar. In this case, omit the 3 tablespoons (50 mL) white wine or liquid as the fresh fruit are juicy.

Maple Upside Down Cake

A 3-minute microwaved upside down cake, tasty and light. The top remains pale yellow, but unmolded it is very attractive.

1 cup (250 mL) maple syrup

2 to 3 tbsp. (30 to 50 mL) chopped nuts (optional)

1 tbsp. (15 mL) soft butter

3 tbsp. (50 mL) sugar

1 egg

1 cup (250 mL) all-purpose flour

2 tsp. (10 mL) baking powder

1/4 tsp. (1 mL) salt

1/4 tsp. (1 mL) nutmeg or cinnamon

1/2 cup (125 mL) milk

Butter an 8 x 8-inch (20 x 20 cm) baking dish. Pour in the maple syrup and nuts to taste. Microwave 3 minutes at HIGH.
Blend together until creamy, the butter, sugar and egg.
Stir together the flour, baking powder, salt, nutmeg or cinnamon. Add to the creamed mixture, alternating with the milk. Stir until well blended. Place as four large balls in the hot syrup, then stretch dough with two forks until all are joined together. This is easy as the dough gets very soft when it comes in contact with the hot syrup, and it joins completely when cooking.
Place pan on a rack, microwave at MEDIUM-HIGH 4 to 5 minutes, or until the top of the cake looks dry and the middle well done. It sometimes happens that the middle looks a little softer, but upon standing on the counter, the residual heat will finish the cooking.
Any leftover may be kept in the baking dish, covered, at room temperature, or unmolded with the syrup on top which penetrates the cake and enhances the flavor. It will keep for several days.

Sliced Apple Cake

A moist cake that I keep a week in its baking pan, covered with plastic wrap, or as long as two weeks refrigerated, either molded or unmolded covered. To serve, I warm up each piece in the serving plate 40 seconds at MEDIUM-HIGH.

2 eggs

3/4 cup (190 mL) brown sugar

1/2 cup (125 mL) vegetable oil

1 tsp. (5 mL) vanilla

3 cups (750 mL) thinly sliced apples, peeled

1¾ cups (435 mL) all-purpose flour

1/2 tsp. (2 mL) salt

1 tsp. (5 mL) baking soda

1/2 tsp. (2 mL) cinnamon

1/2 tsp. (2 mL) nutmeg

1/4 tsp. (1 mL) allspice (optional)

Beat together the eggs and brown sugar. When light, add the oil, vanilla and apples. Mix thoroughly.
Sift together the flour, salt, soda and spices. Add to the apple mixture, blend thoroughly.
Pour into an 8 x 8-inch (20 x 20 cm) ceramic dish. Microwave at HIGH 4 minutes. Let stand 3 minutes, without removing from oven. Microwave 2 to 3 minutes more at MEDIUM-HIGH. Check doneness in the middle of the cake after 2 minutes. Let stand 10 minutes on a rack before unmolding. This cake can also be left in the baking dish and cut into squares as needed. Keep covered.

Lemon Cake (photo opposite p. 49, bottom)
(Convection and microwave)

A simple cake full of flavor with excellent keeping quality. It is one of my favorites.

2 tbsp. (30 mL) butter or margarine	2 tsp. (10 mL) baking powder
1 cup (250 mL) sugar	1/2 cup (125 mL) yogurt
2 eggs	Grated rind of 1 lemon
1¼ cups (300 mL) flour	3 tbsp. (50 mL) sugar
1/2 tsp. (2 mL) salt	Juice of 1 lemon

Beat 2 minutes with the electric mixer the butter or margarine, sugar and eggs. Add the remaining ingredients except the 3 tablespoons (50 mL) sugar and lemon juice. Mix well.
Preheat the convection part of your microwave oven to 325°F. (160°C), place the cake on a rack and bake 45 minutes.
Microwave the lemon juice and the 3 tablespoons (50 mL) sugar together 1 minute at MEDIUM, stir well and pour hot over the cake in the mold as it is removed from the oven.
I leave my cake in the mold, covered, and I cut it as needed. It keeps very well, covered when cooled, with plastic wrap.
This cake may be microwaved, 6 minutes at HIGH, checking doneness after 4 minutes. It is very tasty, but not quite as perfect.

My Mother's Rhubarb Cake

As soon as the first fresh deep pink rhubarb appeared in the springtime garden, Mother made stewed rhubarb and the following cake. It was a treat! In those days we always had **sour milk**. Today, I sour some milk with vinegar or I use buttermilk, or even plain yogurt. When we had guests mother topped the squares of her rhubarb cake with homemade ice cream. How good it was!

1½ cups (375 mL) dark brown sugar	1 tsp. (5 mL) soda
1/2 cup (125 mL) soft butter (unsalted when possible)	1 tsp. (5 mL) salt
	2⅓ cups (580 mL) flour
2 eggs	1½ to 2 cups (375 to 500 mL) rhubarb, washed, peeled and cut into small dice
1 cup (250 mL) sour milk or buttermilk or plain yogurt	

Cream brown sugar and butter of your choice. Use an electric beater or a hand beater. When creamy, add all at once the sour milk, or butter or plain yogurt.
Stir together the soda, salt and flour. Blend into the creamed mixture. Add the rhubarb, stir by hand until well blended with the creamed part.
Grease a 9 x 13-inch (22.5 x 32.5 cm) microwave-safe pan. Microwave 5 minutes at MEDIUM and 3 minutes at HIGH. Check for doneness. Cool on a cake rack.
When cooled unmold. Serve as is or with ice cream or ice with the glaze as in Canadian Carrot Cake.

Leyden Gingerbread
(Convection)

Dutch women have great talent in the use of spices. For centuries, spices have had a priority in their kitchens because of The Netherlands' association with Indonesia. The coriander seeds are fairly easy to find, but they are optional.

1/3 cup (80 mL) pure lard

1/2 cup (125 mL) brown sugar

1 egg

2/3 cup (160 mL) molasses

Grated rind of 1 orange

2½ cups (625 mL) all-purpose flour

2 tsp. (10 mL) baking powder

1/2 tsp. (2 mL) salt

2 tsp. (10 mL) ground ginger

1 tsp. (5 mL) coriander seeds, crushed (optional)

1 tsp. (5 mL) baking soda

1 cup (250 mL) boiling water

Cream together the lard, brown sugar and egg until light and foamy. Add molasses and orange peel. Sift together the flour, baking powder, salt, ginger, crushed coriander seeds and soda. When all is well mixed and creamy, add the boiling water. Mix until well blended. Do not worry if batter seems thin, it should be thin.
Pour into a greased pan. Bake in the convection part of your microwave oven preheated to 325°F. (160°C), 50 to 60 minutes.

Canadian Carrot Cake

Much simpler to make than the Original Swiss Carrot Cake. I make it by the microwave method because the brown sugar and spices sprinkled on top give it a nice finish.

1 cup (250 mL) sugar

3/4 cup (190 mL) vegetable oil*

3 eggs

1½ cups (375 mL) flour

1/2 tsp. (2 mL) salt

1½ tsp. (7 mL) baking soda

1 tsp. (5 mL) cinnamon

1/4 tsp. (1 mL) nutmeg

2 cups (500 mL) carrots, peeled and grated fine

The grated rind of 1/2 a lemon (optional)

Place sugar and vegetable oil in a bowl. Add eggs, one at a time, beating well at each addition. It is important to have this part of the recipe very well beaten (I use an electric hand beater or my mixer). Sift together the flour, salt, soda, cinnamon and nutmeg. Add to the creamed mixture, along with the grated carrots and the lemon rind. Mix the whole until well blended.
Pour into a well greased, microwave-safe 8 x 8-inch (20 x 20 cm) pan. Sprinkle top of cake with 1/2 cup (125 mL) dark brown sugar. Microwave at MEDIUM 5 minutes and 3 minutes at HIGH. Test for doneness. Cool 10 to 15 minutes on rack. Unmold.
Serve as is or use glaze as given after recipe of Swiss Carrot Cake.

* The vegetable oil can be replaced by shortening at room temperature.

Lovers' Apple Cake (photo opposite p. 48)

On Saint Valentine's Day, tie a red ribbon around the cake. Pour on top of the cooled cake, 1/4 to 1/2 cup (60 to 125 mL) hot brandy or rum. No icing, but simply place two red roses on top of the cake.

1/4 cup (60 mL) soft butter

1 cup (250 mL) sugar

1 tsp. (5 mL) vanilla

1 egg

2 cups (500 mL) apples, peeled and cut into small dice

....

1 cup (250 mL) flour

1/2 tsp. (2 mL) each baking powder and baking soda

1 tsp. (5 mL) cinnamon

1/2 tsp. (2 mL) ground cloves

1/2 cup (125 mL) chopped walnuts (optional)

2 tsp. (10 mL) unsweetened or semi-sweet cocoa

Place in a bowl the butter, sugar, vanilla and egg. Beat with an electric mixer, until fluffy and creamy. Stir in the apples. In another bowl, sift together the flour, baking powder, soda, cinnamon and cloves. Add to the creamed mixture. Sprinkle the chopped walnuts over the whole and blend thoroughly. Pour into a square 8-inch (20 cm) ceramic or plastic dish.
Sprinkle top with the cocoa. Place on microwave-safe rack. Microwave 5 minutes at HIGH, let stand 10 minutes in the oven. Check doneness in the middle of the cake. If it is still a little soft, microwave the cake at MEDIUM another 3 minutes.
Cool on rack. Unmold when cooled, or cut into squares and serve.
If you wish to warm up a piece of cake, microwave, set on a plate, 30 to 40 seconds at MEDIUM-HIGH.

Swiss Carrot and Nut cake
(Convection)

The best carrot cake I know. It was made in Switzerland long before we ever heard about it in our part of the world. It can also be made two to three days ahead of time; it remains moist and fresh, as a matter of fact it gains in flavor by mellowing a few days. This original cake has no flour, but very fine breadcrumbs.

1 cup (250 mL) very fine breadcrumbs*

1/2 tsp. (2 mL) cinnamon

1/4 tsp. (1 mL) ground cloves

2/3 cup (160 mL) finely grated carrots, peeled

1¼ cups (315 mL) almonds or filberts, with skins

6 egg yolks, beaten

1¼ cups (315 mL) sugar

Grated rind and juice of 1 lemon

6 egg whites, beaten

How to make fine breadcrumbs in your microwave

Break up 4 to 5 slices of bread, white, brown or raisin bread, place on a microwave-safe rack. Microwave 3 to 5 minutes at HIGH. Start looking at the bread after 3 minutes. It is easy to see how dry it is and give it another minute at a time, if necessary. Let the bread cool on the table or on a plate. This is also quick, 3 to 5 minutes does it. Then make fine breadcrumbs with a rolling pin, or a blender or a food processor.

Measure the needed cup and set aside about 3 spoonfuls for the cake mold. Add the cinnamon and ground cloves to the breadcrumbs in the cup and stir. Set aside. Any leftover breadcrumbs will keep, refrigerated in a covered bowl, for up to 12 months.

Grate the peeled carrots and the nuts, set aside until needed.

How to prepare the pan

Butter bottom and sides of a round 8 or 9-inch (20 or 22.5 cm) cake pan. Sprinkle with the 3 spoonfuls reserved breadcrumbs. Shake all around until butter is all covered, then turn pan over, give it a shake to remove any excess crumbs.

How to make the cake

Combine in a bowl the egg yolks, sugar and lemon juice. Beat with an electrical or hand beater until thick and creamy. Add the breadcrumbs mixed with the cinnamon and cloves. Mix well. Stir in the carrots, the nuts and lemon rind.

Beat the egg whites until stiff. Add 1/3 of the quantity to the batter, mix thoroughly, then fold in carefully the remaining egg whites with a rubber spatula.

Preheat the convection part of your microwave oven to 350°F. (180°C) 15 minutes.

Spoon the batter gently into the prepared pan, place on a rack and bake 45 to 55 minutes, or until a toothpick inserted in the center comes out dry. Cool on rack. Then unmold and wrap in foil. Let the cake ripen 2 to 3 days refrigerated. Serve as is or cover with a glaze made as follows.

The Glaze

This glaze can also be used on a cake of your choice either microwaved or cooked by convection.

2 cups (500 mL) sifted icing sugar

4 tbsp. (60 mL) cold water or orange juice

1/2 tsp. (2 mL) lemon extract or fresh lemon juice

Mix all the ingredients together until very creamy and light, then pour over the cooled cake, smoothing top with a knife, and let dripping fall naturally around the cake.

* The breadcrumbs replace the flour in this cake.

My Finnish friend Marta's Cardamom Cake
(Microwave or Convection)

A delicious sort of pound cake, that I often enjoy, especially in the afternoon with a cup of coffee.

- 1/2 cup (125 mL) soft unsalted butter or margarine
- 1 cup (250 mL) sugar
- 2 eggs
- 1/2 cup (125 mL) molasses
- 2½ cups (625 mL) flour
- 1 tsp. (5 mL) cinnamon

- 1/4 tsp. (1 mL) salt
- 2 tsp. (10 mL) ground cardamom
- 2 tsp. (10 mL) baking soda
- 2 cups (500 mL) commercial sour cream
- 1/2 cup (125 mL) chopped walnuts
- 3/4 cup (190 mL) seedless raisins

Butter two 9 x 5-inch (22.5 x 12.5 cm) pans or a 10-inch (25 cm) Bundt pan.

Cream the butter or margarine at high speed, with electric mixer. Gradually add the sugar, beat until light and creamy. Add eggs, one at a time, beating well at each addition. Add molasses, beat at high speed just enough to blend the whole.

Sift together the flour, cinnamon, salt, cardamom and soda. Add all at once to the creamed mixture and pour the sour cream on top. Then beat at high speed for 2 minutes. Add walnuts and raisins and beat by hand until well mixed into the batter.

Divide the batter equally between the prepared loaf pans or pour into the Bundt pan.

To bake. Microwave in the loaf pans, one at a time, 3 minutes at HIGH, 2 minutes at MEDIUM-HIGH. Test for doneness, because depending on type of oven it may require 2 to 3 minutes more at MEDIUM-HIGH. Cool on rack before unmolding.

The Bundt pan cake. I prefer this large cake baked in the convection part of the microwave preheated at 325°F. (160°C) for 10 minutes. Bake the cake set on a rack, 40 to 50 minutes. Test for doneness. Cool on cake rack. Unmold. Wrap. It will keep fresh in a cool place one or two weeks.

5-Minute Cheesecake (p. 58) →

Original Strawberry Shortcake
(Convection)

A true shortcake is not made with sponge cake, but a sort of rich biscuit type of cake, split, buttered and filled and topped with fresh strawberries. Although it can be microwaved, to be perfect it should be baked in the convection part of the microwave oven.

2 to 3 cups (500 to 750 mL) fresh strawberries	1/2 cup (125 mL) butter
2 cups (500 mL) flour	2 egg yolks
1/4 cup (60 mL) sugar	1/3 cup (80 mL) milk
4 tsp. (20 mL) baking powder	1 cup (250 mL) whipping cream
1/2 tsp. (2 mL) salt	3 tbsp. (50 mL) icing sugar
A good pinch of nutmeg	

Butter generously an 8 or 9-inch (20 or 22.5 cm) round cake pan. Set aside.

Wash and hull the strawberries, drain in a colander while making and baking the shortcake.

Preheat the convection part of your microwave oven to 450°F. (230°C) 15 minutes.

Sift together in a bowl the flour, sugar, baking powder, salt and nutmeg. Cut in the butter, with two knives, and work it into the dry ingredients until the mixture looks mealy.

Beat the egg yolks with the milk. Stir into the flour mixture, stirring only until all the flour has disappeared. Do not try to beat until all is smoothed out.

Spoon batter into the prepared pan. Dip a metal spatula in milk or water and smooth the top of the batter, but it should retain a rugged appearance. Set on a rack and bake about 12 to 14 minutes, or until golden brown on top. When the cooking is tested with the point of a knife, the batter should be dry, when cooked.

Lightly crush the strawberries, add the icing sugar.

Cut the warm shortcake in half, with a sharp knife, butter the bottom of the cake with soft butter, pour the sweetened berries on top. Cover with the other half of the cake.

To taste, sprinkle top with icing sugar and garnish with strawberry halves and whipped cream if the shortcake is eaten at one meal. If not, sprinkle top and strawberries with icing sugar. Serve with a bowl of whipped cream.

Helpful Hint

To toast coconut, place 1/3 cup (80 mL) in a pie plate and microwave at HIGH 1 to 1 1/2 minutes, or until browned.

← Top: Hawaiian Banana Bread (p. 59)
← Bottom: Hélène's Favorite Quick Quick Cake (p. 50)

5-Minute Cheesecake (photo opposite p. 56)

Delicious, creamy, light. Serve it with sweetened strawberries or raspberries or a creamy fresh blueberry sauce. Yummy!

The crust:

1/4 cup (60 mL) butter or margarine

1 cup (250 mL) graham cracker crumbs
   (about 12 biscuits)

2 tbsp. (30 mL) sugar

A good pinch nutmeg

The filling:

An 8-oz (250 g) package cream cheese

1/3 cup (80 mL) sugar

1 egg

1 tbsp. (15 mL) fresh lemon juice

Topping:

1 cup (250 mL) commercial sour cream

3 tbsp. (50 mL) sugar

Microwave butter or margarine in an 8-inch (20 cm) round glass or ceramic pie plate 1/2 to 1 minute at HIGH, until melted. Stir in the graham cracker crumbs, sugar and nutmeg. Mix well and press over bottom and half an inch (1.25 cm) up sides of plate.

In a bowl, microwave cream cheese at MEDIUM, 6 to 8 seconds, or until softened. Stir well. Beat in sugar and egg. Blend in the lemon juice and pour on crust.

Microwave uncovered at HIGH 2 to 3 minutes, or until set around the edges, rotating the dish twice while cooking, unless you have a turntable.

Combine sour cream and sugar for Topping. Spoon over hot cheesecake, spreading with a spatula to completely cover the baked cheese. Microwave at HIGH 1 to 1½ minutes, or until topping is hot. Cool. Refrigerate until ready to serve.

Helpful Hint

To soften cream cheese or butter, microwave a 3-ounce (90 g) package of cream cheese or 1/4 pound (125 g) of butter 20 to 40 seconds at LOW.

Hawaiian Banana Bread (photo opposite p. 57, top)

A few years ago I visited a banana plantation in Hawaii. I was invited afterwards to taste their favorite banana cake and coffee. Both were delicious.

1 cup (250 mL) bananas, mashed	1/2 tsp. (2 mL) baking soda
1/4 cup (60 mL) vegetable oil	1/4 tsp. (1 mL) baking powder
1/4 cup (60 mL) white sugar	1/4 tsp. (1 mL) salt
1/4 cup (60 mL) brown sugar, firmly packed	....
2 eggs	1/2 cup (125 mL) walnuts, chopped
1/2 tsp. (2 mL) each of vanilla and almond extract	....
....	2 tbsp. (30 mL) dark brown sugar
1½ cups (375 mL) flour	1/4 tsp. (1 mL) nutmeg

Beat the first 6 ingredients until creamy and light.
Sift together the next 4 ingredients. Add to the banana mixture. Stir in the walnuts.
Pour the batter into an 8 x 4-inch (20 x 10 cm) microwave-safe loaf pan. (It is not necessary to grease pan).
Blend together the brown sugar and the nutmeg. Sprinkle on top of the cake.
Microwave 4 minutes at HIGH. Move the pan and microwave another 3 minutes at MEDIUM.
Cool cake on a rack for 20 to 30 minutes before unmolding.

Helpful Hint

To heat the liqueur used to flambé a dessert, pour it into a glass container and microwave 15 to 30 seconds at HIGH. Pour over dessert and flambé.

Noël Fruit Cake

This cake will keep for months. When cooled, wrap it first if you wish, in a cloth dipped in rum, wine or whatever you choose, then in aluminum foil and keep in a cool place or refrigerate. When ready to use, let the cake stand at room temperature for 3 to 4 hours before serving.

1/2 lb (250 g) candied cherries, cut up

4 oz (125 g) dates, coarsely chopped

4 oz (125 g) citron peel, chopped

1/2 lb (250 g) candied pineapple, cut up

4 oz (125 g) candied orange peel

4 oz (125 g) seedless raisins

1/2 cup (125 mL) rum or brandy

2 cups (500 mL) walnuts

1 cup (250 mL) Brazil nuts, coarsely chopped or other nuts of your choice

1/2 cup (125 mL) sugar

1 cup (250 mL) all-purpose flour

1 tsp. (2 mL) baking powder

1/4 tsp. (1 mL) salt

1 tsp. (5 mL) ground cardamom

3 tbsp. (50 mL) Dutch cocoa powder (optional)

1/2 cup (125 mL) butter

4 eggs, well beaten

1 tsp. (5 mL) pure vanilla extract

1 tsp. (5 mL) almond extract

Using a large microwave-safe bowl, combine cherries, dates, citron peel, pineapple, orange peel, raisins and rum or brandy. Microwave at HIGH for 2 minutes, to flavor the fruit with the alcohol. Mix in the nuts. Sift together sugar, flour, baking powder, salt and cardamom, and cocoa powder if you wish, and blend into fruit until pieces are well coated.

Cream butter and blend it thoroughly into the fruit mixture.

Combine eggs, vanilla and almond extract, fold into the batter, stirring everything together until well blended. Pour into a buttered glass loaf pan 9 x 5 inches (22.5 x 12.5 cm) or two 8½ x 4½-inch (22 x 11 cm) pans.

Microwave at HIGH 6 to 8 minutes for the larger pan. Test doneness with a wooden pick, if necessary microwave 1 or 2 minutes more, testing again after 1 minute. For two pans, microwave one at a time at HIGH 5 to 6 minutes. Test for doneness as above.

Let stand on kitchen counter. Cake will continue to cook as it cools. Unmold, wrap and store.

Christmas Plum Pudding (photo opposite p. 49, center)

Did you ever bake a Christmas Plum Pudding in 15 minutes, that you can keep well wrapped in a cool place for 10 to 12 months in perfect condition? Try this one. . .

1/2 cup (125 mL) candied fruit	1/2 tsp. (2 mL) each nutmeg, allspice and salt
1 cup (250 mL) raisins	1 cup (250 mL) sugar
1/2 cup (125 mL) currants	1 cup (250 mL) jam or marmalade
1/2 cup (125 mL) rum	2 cups (500 mL) fine breadcrumbs
1 cup (250 mL) minced beef suet	3 eggs
1 tbsp. (15 mL) cinnamon	2 tbsp. (30 mL) milk
2 tsp. (10 mL) ginger	1/2 cup (125 mL) rum, wine or fruit juice

Mix together in a microwave-safe bowl, the candied fruit, raisins, currants and rum. Microwave 2 minutes at HIGH.

Combine in a second bowl, the suet, cinnamon, ginger, nutmeg, allspice, salt, sugar, jam or marmalade and breadcrumbs. Add to the fruit mixture.

Beat together the eggs, milk and wine, rum or fruit juice and blend into the batter. Mix well and pour into one or two microwave-safe bowls. Cover with plastic wrap so pudding steams.

Microwave at MEDIUM-HIGH 8 to 15 minutes, depending on size of bowl used. Microwave one at a time. Test with a wooden pick and microwave 1 minute more if necessary.

Remove plastic wrap and let stand 15 minutes on kitchen counter before unmolding. You may make individual puddings in custard cups and microwave 5 minutes for 6 cups at HIGH. Also test as above.

To glaze: Microwave 1/2 cup (125 mL) jam of your choice at HIGH 15 seconds. Brush over pudding and sprinkle with icing sugar.

To reheat: Place pudding in microwave-safe bowl and reheat 4 to 10 minutes at MEDIUM, according to size.

To flame: Heat 1/3 to 1/2 cup rum 30 seconds at HIGH. Pour over pudding and flame.

To enhance the flavor of your pudding, you may wrap it in a cloth dipped in rum, wine or whatever you choose to let it ripen until Christmas, and up to several months thereafter.

Helpful Hint

To toast sesame seeds, place 1/4 cup (60 mL) sesame seeds in a small bowl. Microwave 2 1/2 to 3 1/2 minutes, stirring twice.

Special Sauces for Plum Pudding

Honey-Ginger Sauce

This original sauce is used on top of a sweet dumpling, but I have enjoyed it for many years on top of plum pudding.

1/2 cup (125 mL) honey

1 cup (250 mL) water or white wine

3 tbsp. (50 mL) grated ginger root

2 tbsp. (30 mL) arrowroot flour or cornstarch

Juice and grated rind of 1 lime

Place all the ingredients in a microwave-safe dish or bowl, stir and microwave 1 minute at HIGH, stir and microwave 3 minutes more at HIGH, stirring once. When sauce is creamy and transparent it is ready.

It may sometimes take 1 minute more, but do it at MEDIUM-HIGH.

Hélène's Mother's Sauce

Hélène has been a constant companion of mine for twenty-eight years, writing, testing, tasting, constantly with a smile, which I have greatly appreciated. With the ginger sauce this is my very favorite to serve with plum pudding.

1 cup (250 mL) sugar

1 cup (250 mL) unsalted butter, softened

4 egg yolks, beaten

1 cup (250 mL) milk or cream

1/4 cup (60 mL) white wine

1/4 cup (60 mL) brandy

Mix together the sugar, butter, beaten egg yolks and milk or cream.

Microwave 3 minutes at MEDIUM, uncovered. Beat well and microwave 1 to 2 minutes, or until sauce has thickened. Add wine and brandy and microwave another 30 seconds. Serve warm or cold, with hot plum pudding.

All About Pies

When eating in a restaurant "Pie" seems to be the great "National Favorite". And this is true virtually the world over.

In France, you will find the bottom crust type; in Italy, it is often an almond crust as well as a pastry type, etc., etc.

In Canada and the USA, no doubt the English double crust pie is the favorite. As for the filling, apples are the winner! For centuries the expression "as easy as pie" has been used. I sometimes wonder about that saying, since only good knowledge and "savoir-faire" concerning pie crust and filling will make it easy. Read carefully the basic instructions regarding pies and if you learn to apply the rules, it will soon become "as easy as pie".

About the flour
A well-made pastry should be tender and flaky. So it is important to know something about the flour.
- All wheat flour contains "gluten", which is a stretchy elastic cell wall that develops as soon as the wheat proteins are mixed with liquid, giving the flour what is needed for a tender and flaky crust pastry.
- All purpose flour and pastry flour are used for pie crust.
- Pastry flour will give a more tender crust, but an all purpose type of good quality also gives satisfactory results.
- All purpose or pastry flour is always specified on the bags. Remember that both can be used.

About the fat in pastry making
1. The use of an unsalted butter or a combination of unsalted butter and a good quality shortening is excellent for a delicate pie — but costly.
2. A pastry made only with high-fat shortening will be good and flaky, but flat in flavor.
3. Pastry made with pure lard which is 100% animal fat, plus a certain percentage of water does make a marvellously tender and flaky pastry.

How to bake a pie in the Microwave
- There are 2 ways to bake the pie:
  a) By the Microwave Method.
  b) By the Convection Method.

The Microwave Method
- Use a microwave-safe plate (Corning or Pyrex or special type plastic).
- The pastry does not brown when baked by the Microwave Method, but the doneness, flavor and texture are quite acceptable.
- Butter the pie plate lightly, line with the pastry of your choice, making sure the dough is firmly set on the edges as well as on the bottom of the pie plate.
- Prick pastry all over with the point of a paring knife or with a fork.
- Place pastry-lined plate on a microwave-safe rack. Microwave 3 to 4 minute at HIGH, depending on the type of pastry you are using, but it could also take 4 to 5 minutes at HIGH.
  It is easy to judge the doneness by the appearance of the pastry. Even though the pastry does not brown when baked by microwave, the flavor and texture are quite acceptable. After all, when the pie crust is filled, it is the texture that is important. I prefer a prebaked single crust for any type of pie when baked by microwave.

The Convection Method
1. Preheat the Convection part of your microwave oven, as required by the recipe.
2. Make the pie according to the recipe. Bake in preheated oven according to the time required by the recipe.
3. Make sure it is placed on a rack.
4. When done, cool on a rack.

Note that a metal pie plate can be used when baking pies by the Convection Method of the microwave oven.

All Purpose Pastry

To prepare this dough, shortening, margarine or butter can be used combined with the pure lard.

2 cups (500 mL) all purpose flour	**About 6 tsp. (90 mL) *very* cold water**
3/4 tsp. (4 mL) salt	**1 tbsp. (15 mL) fresh lemon juice or**
1/3 cup (80 mL) butter	**white vinegar**
1/4 cup (60 mL) pure lard	

Place in a bowl the flour, salt, butter and pure lard. Working quickly and lightly with the tips of your fingers, stir together until mixture resembles grains of rice.

Add the remaining ingredients, combine all lightly, working with the tips of your fingers or a blending fork. As soon as the dough seems to cling together, form into a ball with your hands.

Place in a bowl or wrap in waxed paper, refrigerate 20 to 30 minutes or overnight. Chilling relaxes the dough and prevents shrinking during the baking period, whether baked by the microwave or convection method.

When rolling the dough use as little flour as possible on the board, as too much hardens the pastry.

Honey Apple Pie (p. 70) →

Pure Lard Pastry

My favorite type of pastry. Quickly prepared, it will keep 3 to 4 weeks wrapped in plastic wrap and refrigerated. Or, cover the plastic wrap with foil and freeze, then it will keep for 4 to 6 months.
Cut the ball of dough in four, each package will make a double 8-inch (20 cm) or 9-inch (22.5 cm) pie.

5 cups (1.25 L) all-purpose flour

1 tsp. (5 mL) salt

1 tbsp. (15 mL) sugar

1/4 tsp. (1 mL) baking soda

1 lb (500 g) pure lard

1 egg

3 tbsp. (50 mL) fresh lemon juice or
     white vinegar

Cold water

Stir together in a large bowl, the flour, salt, sugar and baking soda. Mix well and cut in the pure lard with 2 knives, in 2-inch (5 cm) pieces.
Beat together in a 1-cup measure (250 mL) the egg, fresh lemon juice or vinegar and fill with cold water. Add to the flour mixture. Then work the whole with your fingers until you have a nice ball of dough. It is sometimes necessary to add a few tablespoons of cold water. Do so one at a time. Then turn the ball of dough onto a floured table and knead for a minute or two. You will then have a ball of nice soft dough.
It is as easy to roll fresh and soft or refrigerated and cold. The only difference is that the soft type takes a little more flour on the table and rolling pin.

Egg pastry

Interesting pastry which comes out a golden color when baked by microwave. I find it is good with any pie filling.

3 cups (750 mL) all-purpose flour

1 tsp. (5 mL) salt

1 cup (250 mL) butter or margarine

1 egg, lightly beaten

1/2 tsp. (2 mL) grated lemon rind

1/3 cup (80 mL) *ice water*

Place the flour and salt in a large bowl. Stir with a spoon until fluffy and well mixed. Cut in the butter or margarine until the pieces of fat are small.
Mix together the lemon rind and ice water, add to the flour mixture. Stir the whole together with a fork until the dough forms a ball. Refrigerate 30 minutes before rolling.

← Top: Lemon Meringue Pie (p. 76)
← Bottom: Walnut Crust Chocolate Pie (p. 78)

My Homemade Pie Crust Mix

I always keep some ready to be used when in a hurry, in a large empty container for fat or any other container with a tight-fitting lid.

6 cups (1.5 L) all-purpose flour

1 tbsp. (15 mL) salt

1 lb or 2⅓ cups (500 or 580 mL) vegetable shortening*

Mix flour and salt together, then cut in shortening with 2 knives until mixture is crumbly. Pour into container. Cover.
Yield: 9 cups (2.25 L) or 5 or 6 9-inch (22.5 cm) pie shells.
To use: For a one-crust pie measure 1½ cups (375 mL) of mix and 2 to 3 tablespoons (30-50 mL) cold water. Work together with a fork just long enough for the mixture to hold together.
For a 2-crust pie, measure 2¼ cups (560 mL) of the mix with 3 to 4 tablespoons (50 to 60 mL) cold water.
In both cases, the quantity of water may vary with the weather, so, add a little more or less.
Form the dough into a ball, wrap in waxed paper and refrigerate 30 minutes. Roll, form and bake dough as any other type.

* Pure lard can also be used and will give you a more delicate pastry.

French Sweet Pastry for tart shells

A difficult pastry to roll, but surely worth the effort, super with tart shells. Gives a golden color even when only microwaved.

1 cup (250 mL) *sifted* all-purpose or pastry flour

1/8 tsp. (.05 mL) salt

1/4 cup (60 mL) sugar (full)

1 egg yolk, lightly beaten

1/4 cup (60 mL) soft butter

Sift together the flour, salt and sugar. Make a hole in the center, put in the egg yolk and butter. Mix the whole with a fork until smooth. Contrary to other pastry, it must be blended smooth and creamy. Form into a ball, wrap and refrigerate 2 to 3 hours. It is delicate to roll, but it will be appreciated.

Graham Cracker Pie Shell

The recipe is sufficient for a pie shell. It is perfect to bake by microwave.

1 cup (250 mL) graham cracker crumbs

3 tbsp. (50 mL) brown sugar

1 tbsp. (15 mL) honey*

3 tbsp. (50 mL) melted butter
(1 minute at HIGH)

Blend thoroughly the graham cracker crumbs and the brown sugar. Stir in the honey and melted butter. Press into pie plate with your fingers. Refrigerate 1 to 3 hours before filling.

* If the honey is very sugary, uncover and place in microwave 20 to 30 seconds at HIGH. It will then be soft enough to measure easily.

Spiced Crumb Crust

Powdered cinnamon or allspice or cloves is added to the dry ingredients, which changes the flavor. I like cinnamon with apples, allspice with pears, etc.

1/4 cup (60 mL) butter

1¼ cups (310 mL) fine breadcrumbs*

1/2 cup (125 mL) sugar

1/2 tsp. (2 mL) cinnamon or other spice
of your choice

Place the butter in a Pyrex or Corning pie plate. Microwave 1 minute at HIGH. Add remaining ingredients, blend well, with a fork. Then press evenly over bottom and sides of the pie plate. Microwave at HIGH 1 to 1½ minutes. Cool.

* You can use stale bread crushed with a rolling pin or in a blender.

Blender or Food Processor Crunchy Pie Crust

This crust must be prepared in the blender or food processor, otherwise All Bran remains too coarse and tends to harden when microwaved.

1/4 cup (60 mL) butter or margarine	1/4 cup (60 mL) brown sugar
3/4 cup (190 mL) Bran Flakes	1/4 cup (60 mL) walnuts
3/4 cup (190 mL) All Bran	

Microwave butter or margarine in pie plate 1 minute at HIGH.
Place the two brans in blender or food processor with the brown sugar and walnuts, blend on and off until it reaches a coarse texture. Add to melted butter in pie plate. Blend until well mixed. Press evenly on bottom and sides of pie plate.
Place pie plate on a microwave-safe rack and microwave 1 minute at HIGH.
Set aside to cool and fill according to taste.

Helpful Hint

To soften dried fruit, place in a Pyrex dish and sprinkle with water. Cover with plastic wrap and microwave 15 to 30 seconds at HIGH.

Microwaved Open-Face Apple Pie
(also convection)

The first one-crust fruit pie I made in my microwave oven 10 years ago — and I still make it. I have not yet decided whether I prefer cinnamon or ground cardamom seeds as a flavor for the pie. I sometimes use one, then the other.

Pastry or your choice

5 to 6 cups (1.25 to 1.50 L) peeled apples, thinly sliced

1/2 cup (125 mL) white sugar

1/2 cup (125 mL) dark or light brown sugar

3 tbsp. (50 mL) flour

1/4 cup (60 mL) butter

1/2 tsp. (2 mL) salt

1/2 tsp. (2 mL) cinnamon or ground cardamom

2 tbsp. (30 mL) fresh lemon juice or 1/2 tsp. (2 mL) vanilla

1/3 cup (80 mL) light cream or milk

Line the pie plate with the pastry, and microwave according to directions for baking pie shells by microwave.

Fill cooled precooked pie shell with the sliced apples. Blend together the white and brown sugars, the flour, butter, salt, cinnamon or cardamom until you have a crumbly mixture. Pour half this mixture over the apples and stir lightly to blend here and there into the apples, being careful not to puncture the bottom crust. Mix the lemon juice or vanilla with the cream or milk, pour over the apple mixture and top with the remaining crumbs.

There are two ways to bake this pie:

By Microwave

Sprinkle top of pie with a tablespoon (15 mL) of sifted cocoa. Place pie on rack. Microwave 8 to 9 minutes at MEDIUM-HIGH. Let stand 10 minutes in the microwave. Serve hot or cold.

By Convection

Prepare pie as given in the recipe. Preheat the convection part of the microwave oven to 350°F. (180°C) 10 minutes.

Place the pie on a rack. Bake 40 to 50 minutes. Cool on rack, on the kitchen counter.

Molasses Apple Pie
(Convection)

A traditional Canadian apple pie recipe used across Canada.

Pastry of your choice for a 2-crust pie

5 to 6 apples, peeled and sliced or
unpeeled and grated

1/4 cup (60 mL) brown sugar

1/4 cup (60 mL) molasses

2 tbsp. (30 mL) butter or margarine

1/4 tsp. (1 mL) each cinnamon and allspice

Preheat Convection part of your microwave oven to 400°F. (200°C) 20 minutes.
Meanwhile line a 9-inch (22.5 cm) pie plate with pastry.
Mix the apples with the remaining ingredients, fill pie plate. Cover with the top crust. Crimp the edges.
Make a few cuts in the top crust with the point of a knife. Rub dough with a little milk. Place on a rack
in the preheated convection part of the microwave oven. Bake at 400°F. (200°C) about 35 to 45 minutes,
or until a golden color. Serve hot or at room temperature.

Honey Apple Pie (photo opposite p. 64)

One of my favorite apple pies that can be made with one crust or with a bottom and a top crust, the top
crust brushed with sour cream or yogurt and sprinkled with brown sugar. It will have a nice gold crust
cooked by microwave.

Pastry of your choice

5 to 8 apples, peeled, cored and sliced

1/2 cup (125 mL) sour cream or yogurt

1/4 cup (60 mL) honey

1/4 cup (60 mL) light brown sugar

A pinch of salt

1 tsp. (5 mL) cinnamon

1/2 tsp. (2 mL) nutmeg

The grated rind of 1/2 an orange

Line a pie plate with pastry. Fill with the apples. Mix the rest of the ingredients and pour over the
apples. Cover with the top crust, make a few slashes on top. Brush top crust with a bit of sour cream or
yogurt, and sprinkle with about a tablespoon (15 mL) of dark brown sugar.
Place pie on a rack. Microwave at HIGH 8 minutes. Lower heat to MEDIUM and microwave another
5 to 6 minutes. Place on a rack to cool, on the kitchen counter.

Irish Apple Pie
(Convection)

A very popular pie in Ireland, flavored with Irish Whiskey. I often replace the whiskey by an equal quantity of rum more readily available in our kitchen. This pie must be cooked in the convection part of the microwave oven.

6 to 8 apples, peeled and cut in eighths

1/4 cup (60 mL) butter

1 cup (250 mL) sugar

Grated rind and juice of 1 orange

1/4 cup (60 mL) Irish Whiskey or rum

Enough pastry of your choice to cover
   top of dish

Place the butter in an 8 x 8-inch (20 x 20 cm) by 2 inches (5 cm) high baking dish, microwave 2 minutes at HIGH. Add the sugar, orange rind and juice and stir. Stir in the apples and blend well with the flavored butter.
Roll the pastry, cut three holes in it and place over the apples. Press pastry over the edges of the dish, trim if necessary. Preheat the convection part of the microwave oven to 450°F. (230°C) 15 minutes.
Place pie on a rack and bake 30 to 35 minutes, or until the pastry is golden brown.
When the pie is baked, pour the alcohol of your choice equally into each hole on top of the pie, using a funnel.
Serve warm or tepid with thick sour cream or yogurt.

Strawberry Rhubarb Pie
(Microwave and convection)

May and June are the perfect months to enjoy the super flavor of this pie, the favorite of so many. This recipe will show you how to make use of both the microwave and the convection part of your combined microwave oven. It is a one-crust pie.

Pastry of your choice for a 9-inch (22.5 cm)
   pie plate

2 eggs

3/4 cup (190 mL) white sugar

2 tbsp. (30 mL) flour

1/2 cup (125 mL) rich cream

2 cups (500 mL) diced fresh rhubarb

2 cups (500 mL) sliced fresh strawberries

1/4 cup (60 mL) brown sugar

1/4 cup (60 mL) flour

The grated rind of 1/2 an orange

2 tbsp. (30 mL) butter

Roll pastry and line pie plate. Any type of pastry can be used. Beat together until smooth, the eggs, white sugar, 2 tablespoons (30 mL) flour and cream. Stir in the rhubarb and strawberries. Pour into the pie shell. Mix in a bowl the brown sugar, the 1/4 cup (60 mL) flour, the grated rind of the orange and the butter. When mixture is crumbly, sprinkle over the fruits in the pie shell. Place on a rack, microwave 9 minutes at HIGH. Remove pie plate from microwave.
Preheat the convection part of the microwave oven to 425°F. (210°C) 10 minutes. Place pie on rack, bake 20 to 25 minutes or until crust is golden brown and the filling creamy.

Blueberry Pie (photo overleaf)
(Convection)

Blueberry pie has a sort of old-fashioned air. In season I usually try to make this pie at least twice. This is my mother's recipe. I have never found a tastier one.

Pastry of your choice for a 2-crust pie

4 well-packed cups (1 L) fresh blueberries

1/2 cup (125 mL) white sugar

1/2 cup (125 mL) light brown sugar

1/3 cup (80 mL) maple syrup or sugar

4 tbsp. (60 mL) flour

3 tbsp. (50 mL) cornstarch or rice flour

1/4 tsp. (1 mL) allspice

1/4 tsp. (1 mL) nutmeg

3 tbsp. (50 mL) melted butter

2 tbsp. (30 mL) lemon juice

Line a pie plate with the rolled pastry. Brush crust with a little melted butter. Mix all the ingredients thoroughly. Pour into pie shell. Top with pastry. Sprinkle top with a tablespoon (15 mL) sugar. Preheat the convection part of your microwave oven to 400°F. (200°C) 10 minutes. Place pie on a rack. Bake 35 to 40 minutes, or until golden brown.

The Best of Pumpkin Pies (photo overleaf)
(Convection)

When fresh pumpkin is not available, I use canned pumpkin. There is no need to pre-bake the bottom crust for this pie. Easy and quick to make.

2 cups (500 mL) cooked pumpkin or squash

1/2 cup (125 mL) sugar

2 eggs, lightly beaten

1/4 tsp. (1 mL) salt

1½ cups (375 mL) milk

1/4 cup (60 mL) molasses

2 tbsp. (30 mL) melted butter

1 tsp. (5 mL) ginger

1/2 tsp. (2 mL) nutmeg

1 tsp. (5 mL) cinnamon

Pastry of your choice for a 9-inch (22.5 cm) 2-crust pie

Preheat Convection part of your microwave oven to 400°F. (200°C) 20 minutes.
Mix all the ingredients of the pie in a bowl. Stir well.
Line a pie plate with the rolled pastry. Fill with pumpkin or squash mixture. Top with another rolled pastry. Crimp the edges. Make a few cuts in the top crust with the point of a knife. Brush top with a little cream or milk. Place on a rack in the preheated oven. Bake at 400°F. (200°C) 30 to 35 minutes. Serve at room temperature.

Cranberry Muffins (p. 83) →

Rum Raisin Pie
(Convection)

Heating the rum and raisins in the microwave at HIGH for 3 minutes makes them soft, rummy and delicious. The rum may be replaced by fresh orange juice.

3/4 cup (190 mL) seedless raisins

1/4 cup (60 mL) rum or fresh orange juice

1 egg

1 tsp. (5 mL) cornstarch

1/2 cup (125 mL) sugar

1/2 cup (125 mL) commercial sour cream

1/4 tsp. (1 mL) cardamom or cinnamon

1 tbsp. (15 mL) fresh lemon juice

Pastry for a 9-inch (225 cm) pie shell

Place the raisins, rum or fresh orange juice in a cup or a bowl. Microwave at HIGH 3 minutes. Let stand until just cooled. Place the egg, cornstarch, sugar, sour cream, cardamom or cinnamon and fresh lemon juice in a bowl, stir until well mixed. Microwave at MEDIUM-HIGH 2 minutes, stir well and microwave another minute or two at MEDIUM-HIGH, or until creamy. Stir well, add the rum-soaked raisins, mix well and let stand while the pastry is baked.

Place baking rack in lower part of your oven. Preheat convection part of your microwave oven to 400°F. (200°C), 15 minutes. Line a 9-inch pie plate with the rolled pastry. Crimp the edges. Cover with a square of waxed paper, pour in a cup of uncooked rice.* Put the prepared pie plate on the rack, bake 5 to 8 minutes, remove pie plate from oven, gently pick up the waxed paper with the rice and return pie shell to oven until golden brown, about 5 to 10 minutes more. Cool. When cooled, fill with the rum raisin filling.

Let stand about one hour at room temperature. Serve.

This rice method prevents the pastry from shrinking in the plate.

Helpful Hint

For fresh coffee any time, refrigerate leftover coffee and microwave in a large cup 1 1/2 to 2 minutes at HIGH.

← Bottom: Blueberry Pie (p. 72) and The Best of Pumpkin Pies (p. 72)

Spring Lemon Mincemeat
(Convection)

Every year I make some of my spring mincemeat. It will keep 6 months in a cool place or in the refrigerator.

1/2 cup (125 mL) fresh lemon juice	1/2 tsp. (2 mL) salt
3 cups (625 mL) grated unpeeled apples	2 tsp. (10 mL) cinnamon
1 cup (250 mL) raisins of your choice	1 tsp. (5 mL) ground cloves
1/2 cup (125 mL) nuts of your choice, chopped	1 tsp. (5 mL) ginger
1/4 cup (60 mL) marmalade of your choice	1 tsp. (5 mL) ground cardamom (optional)
2 cups (500 mL) sugar	The grated rind of 2 oranges

Combine all the ingredients in the order given. Mix thoroughly. Keep in glass jar, covered. Refrigerate.
To Bake a Lemon Mincemeat Pie by the Convection Method, add 1/4 cup (60 mL) melted butter for each 2 cups (500 mL) of the mincemeat used.
Line a pie plate with a pastry of your choice. Fill with mincemeat. Bake in the convection part of the microwave oven preheated to 400°F. (200°C) 10 minutes. Place pie on a rack. Bake 30 to 40 minutes or until golden brown.
Serve warm topped with ice cream or serve cooled but not refrigerated.

Elizabeth's Christmas Mincemeat
(Convection)

If you like a mincemeat without any spices, this one is for you. It will keep in perfect condition, well covered and refrigerated, up to one year.

1 lb (500 g) currants	1/2 lb (250 g) suet, minced
1 lb (500 g) raisins	1/2 lb (250 g) mixed peel
1 lb (500 g) apples, peeled and chopped (about 5 medium apples)	The rind and juice of 2 lemons
1 lb (500 g) sugar	1/2 cup almonds (optional)

Mix all the ingredients together thoroughly. Place in well covered containers and refrigerate.
To make a pie, just line a pie plate with the pastry of your choice, and fill with about 2 cups (500 mL) of mincemeat, more or less according to your taste. You may top the mincemeat with one apple, peeled and sliced, and sprinkle a few spoonfuls of rum or brandy over all. Cover with dough.
Place the pie on a rack in the convection part of your microwave oven preheated 10 minutes at 400°F. (200°C). Bake 30 to 40 minutes or until golden brown.

Lean Mincemeat

In the old days, when no household dared be without homemade mincemeat, this meatless type was the great favorite. I have been making it for years and have kept it in my cold pantry for as long as a year, or refrigerated for up to two years, and have never lost even a spoonful of it.

1 large orange
1 large lemon
2 cups (500 mL) seeded raisins
2 cups (500 mL) golden raisins
1 cup (250 mL) pitted dates, chopped
10 medium-sized apples (a firm apple is best)
1½ cups (375 mL) apple cider or juice
3 cups (750 mL) firmly packed brown sugar

1 tsp. (5 mL) salt
1 tsp. (5 mL) allspice
1 tsp. (5 mL) nutmeg
1 tsp. (5 mL) ground cloves
2 tsp. (10 mL) ground cardamom (optional)
1 tbsp. (15 mL) vanilla or
    1/4 cup (60 mL) rum or brandy (optional)

Slice orange and lemon, unpeeled, remove the seeds, cut slices in half and pass through a food processor or a blender until chopped fine. Place in a large microwave-safe dish, add the raisins and the dates. Stir to mix. Do not peel the apples, but remove cores and seeds, cut into small dice. Add to the orange-lemon mixture. Add the apple cider or juice. Stir until well mixed. Microwave, uncovered, 20 minutes at HIGH. Stir thoroughly and microwave another 10 minutes at MEDIUM. Add the brown sugar, salt, spices and vanilla. Stir until well mixed. Microwave at MEDIUM 5 minutes. Add the rum or brandy. Stir thoroughly. Cool for about 15 minutes.

Pack into glass jars. Cover tightly and put aside to ripen, or use when cooled.

Helpful Hint

To dry orange or lemon rind, place it in a pie plate and microwave 1/2 to 1 minute at HIGH. Stor once.

Lemon Meringue Pie (photo opposite p. 65, top)
(Microwave and convection)

This recipe will show you how to proceed when both oven functions, microwave and convection, are to be used for the same recipe.

Filling:

1 cup (250 mL) sugar

1¼ cups (315 mL) cold water

1 tbsp. (15 mL) butter

1/4 cup (60 mL) cornstarch

3 tbsp. (50 mL) cold water

The grated rind of 1/2 a lemon

The juice of 1 lemon

3 egg yolks

2 tbsp. (30 mL) milk

Pastry of your choice for a 9-inch (22.5 cm)
   pie shell

Combine in a bowl the sugar, the 1¼ cups (315 mL) cold water and the butter. Microwave at HIGH 3 to 4 minutes or until sugar is dissolved, stirring once.

Mix the cornstarch with the 3 tablespoons (50 mL) cold water. Add to the above, stirring well. When mixed, microwave at HIGH 2 minutes, stir, and microwave at HIGH another 2 to 4 minutes or until creamy, stirring once or twice. Add the lemon rind and juice, stir. Beat the egg yolks with the milk. Add to above mixture. Microwave at MEDIUM-HIGH 3 to 4 minutes, stirring twice. If necessary, to obtain a creamy filling microwave another minute or two. Cool while baking the pie shell.

Place a rack in your oven. Preheat convection part of your microwave to 400°F. (200°C) 20 minutes. Line a pie plate with the rolled pastry. Cover with a square of waxed paper, pour in a cup of uncooked rice.*

Place pie plate in preheated oven. Bake 5 to 8 minutes at 400°F. (200°C). Remove plate from oven, gently pick up the waxed paper with the rice and put shell back into the oven, bake until golden brown all over, or about 8 to 10 minutes more. Cool. Pour cooled filling into cooled pie shell.

The Meringue:

3 egg whites

6 tbsp. (90 mL) sugar

1 tsp. (5 mL) fresh lemon juice or
   1/4 tsp. (1 mL) vanilla

A pinch of salt

Beat the egg whites with a whisk or an egg beater until they form soft peaks when lifting the beater. Then, gradually add the remaining ingredients, one at a time, beating well at each addition.

Spread over the lemon filling, making sure it is spread to the edges of the filling. Place pie with meringue on rack.

Brown at 400°F. (200°C) until golden brown, about 15 to 20 minutes. Cool and serve. Do not refrigerate.

* *This rice method prevents the pastry from shrinking in the plate.*

Sugar Pie
(Convection)

There is no need to pre-cook the crust of this pie. A most popular winter dessert.

A 9-inch (22.5 cm) unbaked pie shell

1 cup (250 mL) brown sugar

1/4 cup (60 mL) all-purpose flour

1 cup (250 mL) milk

1 cup (250 mL) cream

1 tbsp. (5 mL) maple extract

3 tbsp. (50 mL) butter or margarine

A good pinch of nutmeg

Preheat Convection part of your microwave oven to 400°F. (200°C) 20 minutes.
Line a pie plate with the unbaked pie shell of your choice.
Mix the brown sugar and flour, spread in the bottom of the pastry. Mix the cream, milk and maple extract, pour over the brown sugar. Dot with butter.
Place on a rack in the preheated oven and bake 30 to 35 minutes, or until the crust is golden brown. Cool and serve.

Bernard's Favorite
(Convection)

My husband and I both eat quite a bit of cottage cheese and yogurt. One day I tried a pie with cottage cheese, and it became a favorite. Use a pastry of your choice or a graham cracker crust.

Pie shell of your choice

1/2 cup (125 mL) jam of your choice

1½ cups (375 mL) cottage cheese

1 tbsp. (15 mL) flour

1/4 tsp. (1 mL) salt

1 cup (250 mL) heavy or light cream

1/3 cup (80 mL) sugar

3 eggs, separated

The grated rind of a lemon

2 tbsp. (30 mL) fresh lemon juice

Line the pie plate with pastry of your choice or follow recipe on page. . . for Graham Cracker Pie Shell. Spread the jam of your choice in the bottom of the pie crust. Blend together the remaining ingredients, except the egg whites. Beat the egg whites until stiff, and fold into the cottage cheese mixture. Pour the whole over the jam.
Bake by convection. Preheat the convection part of the microwave oven to 400°F. (200°C) for 10 minutes.
Place pie on a rack, reduce heat to 350°F. (180°C) and bake about 35 minutes or until mixture is firm when tested with the blade of a knife. Serve hot or at room temperature.

Walnut Crust Chocolate Pie (photo opposite p. 65, bottom)

If you are looking for a very special dessert, though slightly expensive, that can be made 6 to 12 hours ahead of time, try this pie.

Crust:

1¼ cups (310 mL) walnuts, finely minced

2 tbsp. (30 mL) brown sugar

2 tbsp. (30 mL) soft butter

Filling:

6 tbsp. (90 mL) butter

4 oz (112 g) unsweetened chocolate

1 cup (250 mL) sugar

3 eggs, lightly beaten

2 tbsp. (30 mL) brandy

1 tsp. (5 mL) vanilla extract

A pinch of salt

If you have a blender or food processor, use it to mince the walnuts fine but not powdered, a sharp knife can be used but it takes longer. Blend the chopped walnuts, brown sugar and the 2 tablespoons (30 mL) soft butter. Press mixture into an 8-inch or 9-inch (20 or 22.5 cm) pie plate, covering evenly the bottom and the side of the plate. Microwave at HIGH 1 minute. Mix together the 6 tablespoons (90 mL) butter, the unsweetened chocolate and sugar. Microwave 2 minutes at HIGH. Stir, if the chocolate is not all melted microwave one more minute at HIGH. Stir well and add the lightly beaten eggs*, brandy, vanilla and salt. Stir until well blended. Pour into cooled pie shell. Refrigerate at least 4 to 5 hours before serving.

* The eggs are added raw to first mixture that is hot, then well beaten they cook without any further heat. If possible, have them 1 hour at room temperature before use.

Meringue Pie
(Convection)

Four egg whites and a little time, and you have a beautiful tasty meringue pie. Both meringue and filling can be done in the morning and put together when ready to be served for dinner.
The meringue base of this pie **must** be cooked in the convection part of your microwave oven. The filling can be microwaved before or after baking the meringue base.

Meringue:

4 egg whites

A good pinch of cream of tartar

A pinch of salt

1/4 tsp. (1 mL) vanilla extract

3/4 cup (190 mL) sugar

If you have a cake mixer, by all means use it as it makes all of it so easy, or use a hand beater.
Beat the egg whites in a bowl until frothy. Add the cream of tartar and keep on beating for about half a minute. Add the salt and vanilla and beat again at MEDIUM-HIGH speed, while adding the sugar half a teaspoon (2 mL) at a time, until the whites form shiny firm peaks. This should take about 5 minutes in a mixer. Oil bottom, sides and rim of a 9 or 10-inch (22.5 or 25 cm) Pyrex or Corning pie plate. Mound meringue in the pie plate, using a rubber spatula to bring the meringue to the edges of the plate. If you can, place the meringue about 1½ inches (4 cm) above the rim of the plate, which gives you a deep pie that can be filled generously when cooked.
Preheat convection part of microwave oven to 200°F. (100°C) 10 minutes. Place meringue plate on a rack. Bake 2 hours. Let it cool on wire rack in the oven (if you do not need your oven), or on the kitchen counter.

Cream Filling for Meringue Pie

Little changes are to be made to this basic cream to produce a different pie each time. Following are a few of them, you can easily create your own from it.

4 egg yolks

1/2 cup (125 mL) sugar

1 tablespoon (15 mL) fresh lemon juice

3 tablespoons (50 mL) of a liqueur
  of your choice

1 cup (250 mL) heavy cream, whipped

Toasted thinly sliced almonds, to garnish

In a 4-cup (1 L) measuring cup, combine the egg yolks and sugar. Mix well. I use a wire whisk, which makes the work quick and easy.
Microwave at MEDIUM 2 minutes, beating after 1 minute of cooking. Beat again after another minute and microwave 1 minute more, if necessary. It should have the consistency of mayonnaise. Slow cooking and lots of stirring are necessary to prevent the eggs from turning. When creamy, remove from microwave, add lemon juice, mix, add liqueur, mix well. Cool.
Whip the cream and fold into the cooled yolk mixture. Mix well. Pour into the cold meringue shell, sprinkle top with toasted almonds and refrigerate at least 3 hours.
Toasted Almonds — Place 1/3 cup (80 mL) thinly slivered almonds on a plate. Microwave at HIGH 3 to 4 minutes, stirring twice, or until almonds are golden brown. Cool for 10 minutes and sprinkle over top of cream in the pie.

Variations on Liqueur

Mint Liqueur, a dash of green coloring added to the filling
OR
In the summer, chop very fine 1/2 cup (125 mL) fresh mint leaves and use to replace liqueur called for in the recipe.
Raspberry. Give the cream a pale pink shade with a bit of red food coloring. Top with fresh raspberries, enough to completely cover the cream. Very attractive when placed in a circle on the cream.
Orange cream. Add 2 tablespoons (30 mL) Grand Marnier or Cointreau to the filling. Add 2 drops each of red and yellow coloring for a pale yellow color.
Chocolate Cream. Melt 2 to 3 ounces (56-74 g) of semi-sweet chocolate. Place the wrapped squares on a plate. Microwave about 2 minutes at HIGH. It is then easy to scrape from the paper the melted chocolate and to add it to the filling. To taste, garnish top of pie with a few grated slivers of semi-sweet chocolate.
Rum Raisin Cream. Place in a bowl 1/2 cup (125 mL) raisins of your choice and 4 tablespoons (60 mL) rum. Microwave 1 minute at HIGH. Cool. Mix with the basic cream filling. Pour into cooked cooled meringue base. Garnish top with little fans of thinly sliced unpeeled oranges.

Muffins

Freshly baked, hot muffins are very popular. They may be served as a breakfast muffin, enjoyed for a snack anytime during the day, whether warmed up or buttered. Their plus — they are marvellously easy to blend and bake, with almost endless variations! All types of muffins will warm up in 6 to 9 seconds at HIGH, for 1 or 2.

Important "Know-How"
- The liquid ingredients should be measured in one bowl.
- The dry ingredients should be measured in another bowl.
- The **liquid** ingredients should be poured **all at once,** over the dry ingredients.
- Then, the liquid ingredients are stirred into the dry ingredients until they are moistened but still lumpy.
- As the batter should never be beaten, it should be worked quickly. So, be sure to have everything ready, even the molds.
- Butter the molds or spray lightly with "PAM", or use muffin paper cups placed in a plastic muffin mold.
- Muffins **do not** brown in the microwave, although they cook to perfection, plus cooking very fast.

To brown, use one of the following topping ideas:
- brown sugar mixed with a teaspoon (5 mL) of cocoa, simply sprinkled on top of each muffin, or
- cinnamon sugar or chocolate chips or a little swirl of red jam on top of the batter makes them attractive, or cranberry sauce, etc.
- muffin paper cups placed in each section of a muffin pan is the easiest and most attractive way to serve microwaved muffins.
- Do not use muffin pans with steam vent holes in the bottom without paper cups, as it is impossible to take them to the microwave oven without having some of the batter drip through the holes.

When the recipe contains brown sugar or molasses, the muffins will brown naturally.

Basic Muffins I

I have two favorite basic microwaved muffin recipes that can be varied almost endlessly. Use your own ideas or preferences once you know how to make them.

The 2-egg Batter	3 tbsp. (50 mL) sugar
2 cups (500 mL) flour	2 eggs
2½ tsp. (12 mL) baking powder	3/4 cup (190 mL) cold milk
1/2 tsp. (2 mL) salt	1/4 cup (60 mL) melted butter or margarine

Sift together in a bowl, the flour, baking powder, salt and sugar.
Beat together the eggs and milk, pour over the flour mixture, stir to just moisten the dry ingredients.
Melt the butter 2 minutes at HIGH.
Pour over the batter and stir until the dry ingredients are thoroughly moistened but still lumpy, in other words, just enough to blend the two. Pour into prepared muffin pans, only 2/3 full.
To taste, sprinkle top lightly with finely chopped nuts or cinnamon and sugar mixed together or toasted coconut*, or a teaspoon (5 mL) each of brown sugar and cocoa mixed together.
For 6 muffins, microwave at HIGH 2 to 2½ or 3 minutes. The variation in baking time depends on the type of muffins. Serve hot.

* To toast coconut in the microwave oven, simply place the required coconut in a plate. Microwave 2 to 3 minutes at HIGH, stirring twice. Do not brown too much, it will brown more when the muffins are microwaved.

Tea-time Currant Dainties (p. 87) →

Basic Muffins II

The ingredients and the quantities are almost the same as for Muffins I. Yet when baked they are different. I was never able to decide which one I prefer, I sometimes make No. I, other times, No. II.

The 1-egg Batter
1²/₃ cups (410 mL) flour
1/2 cup (125 mL) sugar
2 tsp. (10 mL) baking powder
1/2 tsp. (2 mL) salt

1/4 tsp. (1 mL) nutmeg or cinnamon or allspice
1/3 cup (80 mL) vegetable oil
3/4 cup (190 mL) milk
1 egg

Combine in a bowl the flour, sugar, baking powder, salt, nutmeg or cinnamon or allspice. Stir until well mixed.
Mix together the oil, milk and egg. Pour into dry ingredients and stir just enough to moisten the dry ingredients.
For a topping, choose one of the "topping ideas" on page... Microwave 6 muffins 2½ to 3 minutes at HIGH.
Variations which can be used with either Basic Muffins.
Cheese Muffins: Add 1/2 cup (125 mL) grated cheese of your choice to the dry ingredients.
Bacon Muffins: Microwave 4 to 6 slices of bacon on a piece of white towelling 4 minutes at HIGH. Cool and crumble. **Omit** sugar in the muffin recipe and add the cooked crumbled bacon to the dry ingredients.
Health Muffins: Replace 1 cup (250 mL) of the flour called for in the recipe by 1 cup (250 mL) wholewheat or graham or buckwheat flour. Use dark brown sugar instead of white sugar in the same quantity as called for in the basic recipe. Bake same as for plain muffins.
Apple Muffins: Add 1 cup (250 mL) peeled and finely chopped apples to dry ingredients.
Dried Fruit Muffins: Use brown sugar in batter instead of the white sugar, and add 1/4 to 1/2 cup (60 to 125 mL) dried currants or raisins or soft dried diced apricots or dried chopped apples.
Oatmeal Muffins: Replace 1 cup (250 mL) flour by 1 cup (250 mL) quick-cooking oatmeal.
Sour Cream Muffins: I love these! Use 1 to 1¼ cups (250 to 315 mL) commercial sour cream in place of milk and melted butter.
Decrease baking powder to 1/2 teaspoon (2 mL) and add 1/2 tsp. (2 mL) soda.
Jam Muffins: Make batter of your choice. Microwave 2 minutes at HIGH. Quickly place 1 teaspoon (5 mL) of a jam of your choice and 2 teaspoons (10 mL) finely chopped nuts (optional) on top of each muffin. Microwave 30 to 40 seconds at HIGH.

← **Left: Carrot and Pineapple "Petits Fours" (p. 90)**
← **Top right: Quick Blueberry Muffins (p. 82)**
← **Bottom right: Jam Squares (p. 88)**

Bran Muffins

I sometimes use all natural bran or I mix half bran flakes and half natural bran. These are butterless, perfect for a fat free diet.

3 cups (750 mL) natural whole bran

1/2 cup (125 mL) dark brown sugar

1 tsp. (5 mL) baking soda

1½ cups (375 mL) flour

2 cups (500 mL) buttermilk or sour milk

Place the bran and brown sugar in a bowl and stir to mix. Sift together the baking soda and flour. Add to bran mixture with the buttermilk or sour milk. Stir just enough to blend. Pour into muffin pan. Microwave 4 to 5 minutes at HIGH. Serve hot with honey.

Quick Blueberry Muffins (photo opposite p. 81, top right)

I make these all year round. In the summer, I use fresh blueberries, in the winter, I replace them with my own frozen blueberries. There is hardly any difference between the two, if you freeze your own blueberries.*

1½ cups (375 mL) flour

1/2 cup (125 mL) sugar

2½ tsp. (12 mL) baking powder

1/4 tsp. (1 mL) salt

1 egg

3/4 cup (190 mL) milk

1/3 cup (80 mL) melted butter

1 cup (250 mL) blueberries

Grated rind of 1/2 a lemon

2 tbsp. (30 mL) sugar

Sift together the flour, sugar, baking powder and salt.
In another bowl, beat the egg, add the milk and the melted butter. Pour over the dry ingredients, stir just enough to moisten the whole. Stir in the blueberries.
Spoon into microwave-safe muffin pan lined with paper baking cups. Mix together the lemon rind and sugar. Sprinkle a bit on each muffin. For a 6-muffin mold, microwave at HIGH 2 to 2½ minutes. Test doneness. If necessary, microwave another minute at MEDIUM.

* *To freeze your own blueberries: Wash them and dry them on a cloth. Place 1 teaspoon (5 mL) sugar in the bottom of each container or freezer bag. (Do not freeze more than 2 cups (500 mL) per container). Place prepared berries on top of sugar. Do not mix. Cover with a little square of crumpled waxed paper. Cover container or close bag. Freeze. Prepared this way, the thawed out blueberries look like fresh ones.*

All-Season Blueberry Muffins

In the winter, I replace the fresh blueberries with frozen blueberries, not even thawed, **or** with an equal quantity of well drained crushed pineapple.

1/4 cup (60 mL) butter

3 tbsp. (50 mL) margarine

2/3 cup (160 mL) sugar

1 egg, lightly beaten

1 cup (250 mL) milk

1½ cups (375 mL) fresh blueberries

2¼ cups (560 mL) all-purpose flour

1 tsp. (5 mL) salt

4 tsp. (20 mL) baking powder

Cream together the butter, margarine and sugar. When light and creamy, add the egg and the milk, beat until well blended. Add the blueberries.
Sift together the flour, salt and baking powder. Add all at once to the creamed mixture. Mix **just enough** to blend and fold in the blueberries.
Pour into muffin pan. Top each muffin with 3 to 4 blueberries. Microwave 4 to 5 minutes at HIGH, or until done. Serve with butter whipped until creamy and top with sweetened blueberries; this is optional.

Cranberry Muffins (photo opposite p. 72)

I found this recipe in the "Farm Journal" which I read faithfully. I keep on making them. They have a sort of Christmas feeling.

1 cup (250 mL) fresh cranberries

1/4 cup (60 mL) sugar

1½ cups (375 mL) flour

1/4 cup (60 mL) sugar

2 tsp. (10 mL) baking powder

1 tsp. (5 mL) salt

1/2 tsp. (2 mL) cinnamon

1/4 tsp. (1 mL) allspice

1 egg, beaten

The grated rind of 1/2 an orange

3/4 cup (190 mL) orange juice

1/3 cup (80 mL) butter

1/4 cup (60 mL) chopped nuts of your choice (optional)

Coarsely chop raw cranberries on a piece of waxed paper, with a sharp knife. Pour into a bowl and sprinkle with 1/4 cup (60 mL) of the sugar, set aside.
Place in a bowl the flour, the remaining 1/4 cup (60 mL) sugar, baking powder, salt, cinnamon and allspice. Make a well in the center of the mixed dry ingredients.
Combine the egg, grated orange rind and orange juice. Melt the butter 1 minute at HIGH, add to the orange juice mixture.
Pour the whole all at once into the flour mixture. Stir just enough to blend. Fold in the chopped sweetened cranberries.
Fill muffin pans a little more than half. Microwave at HIGH 3 to 4 minutes, or until dry on top.

Super Strawberry or Raspberry Muffins

In the summer, I use about 1½ cups (375 mL) of fresh strawberries or raspberries, that I add to the batter. It does not change the baking time.

1¾ cups (440 mL) flour	1/3 cup (80 mL) vegetable oil
1/3 cup (80 mL) sugar	1 egg
2 tsp. (10 mL) baking powder	1 package (425 mL) frozen strawberries or raspberries, thawed
1/2 tsp. (2 mL) salt	

Make sure the muffin pan is well oiled or use cupcake paper cups. Place in mixing bowl the flour, sugar, baking powder and salt. Mix together in another bowl the oil, egg and 1 cup (250 mL) of the strawberries or raspberries and juice. Add to the dry ingredients and stir just enough to moisten the whole.

Fill the muffin pans only half full with the batter. Microwave at HIGH 2½ to 3 minutes or until done. Serve with the stawberry or raspberry butter.

Strawberry or Raspberry Butter: Blend together 1/2 cup (125 mL) soft butter or margarine and the remaining strawberries or raspberries and their juice. Refrigerate and use to butter top of hot muffins when ready to serve.

Upside Down Muffins
(Microwave or Convection)

These super and unusual muffins must be baked in a microwave-safe muffin pan without holes. They are a sort of upside down muffin. They are also very good baked in the convection part of the microwave oven, which permits you to use any metal muffin pan of your choice.

2 tbsp. (30 mL) butter	1/2 tsp. (2 mL) salt
1/2 cup (125 mL) maple syrup	3 tbsp. (50 mL) maple syrup
1/4 cup (60 mL) walnuts, coarsely chopped	1 cup (250 mL) milk
2 cups (500 mL) flour	1/4 cup (60 mL) vegetable oil
3 tsp. (15 mL) baking powder	1 egg
1 tsp. (5 mL) cinnamon or allspice	

Place butter and the 1/2 cup (125 mL) maple syrup in a measuring cup. Microwave 3 minutes at HIGH. Place 1 teaspoon (5 mL) in the bottom of each muffin pan. Then sprinkle 1 teaspoon (5 mL) of chopped walnuts over the syrup.

Sift together in a large bowl the flour, baking powder, cinnamon or allspice and the salt.

Stir together the 3 tablespoons (50 mL) maple syrup, milk, oil and egg. Pour into the dry ingredients all at once and stir just until moistened.

Fill each cup only 2/3 full over the syrup.

By Convection: Preheat convection part of your microwave oven 5 minutes at 425°F. (225°C). Place muffin pan on rack and bake 20 minutes, or until golden brown.

Microwaved: Microwave at HIGH 2½ to 3 minutes, for 6 muffins.

As soon as muffins are baked by either method, unmold on a sheet of waxed paper, otherwise the syrup will harden.

Cookies

How to on cookies

Regardless of the type of cookies you wish to make, read the following to be assured of perfect success.

1. Cookies can be baked by microwave or in the convection part of your microwave oven.
2. Read your recipe, then place near you all the utensils and ingredients that are required.
3. **Make sure all ingredients** are at room temperature.
4. When the cookies are to be baked in the convection part of your microwave oven, preheat the oven 15 minutes to the degree of heat demanded by the recipe.
5. **Rolled cookies** If you have to roll the cookie dough in sheets or strips, etc., the flour used for dusting the table should be used sparingly, and any flour remaining on the cut cookies should be brushed off before putting them on the baking sheet.
   When making this type of cookie, they will be easier to roll if refrigerated before rolling the dough.
6. **Sheet Cookies** are quick and easy to prepare, but when time permits, they will be perfect in texture and flavor if they are refrigerated an hour or so before being rolled.
7. **When baking any type of cookie,** always give careful attention to the baking time, which can be a minute more or less, depending on the temperature of the ingredients, some may be cool, or cold, or at room temperature, or whether pastry or all-purpose flour has been used, etc.
8. **To keep cookies crisp** Keep in a container with a loose cover. Pack cookies with a sheet of waxed paper between each row. Keep in a cool place when possible.
9. **To keep cookies soft** Use an airtight container, pack cookies as above with a sheet of waxed paper between each row. Place 3 to 4 slices of unpeeled apple on the top sheet. Change the slices from time to time to ensure freshness.

Here are a few of my favorite, easy to make, cookies.

Brown Sugar Bars

If your brown sugar has hardened, add a few drops of water, about 1/4 teaspoon (1 mL) on top of the sugar, whatever the quantity, microwave 10 to 15 seconds at HIGH. Surprise, you will find it is very easy to measure. Repeat operation if it hardens again.

1/2 cup (125 mL) butter	**1/4 tsp. (1 mL) salt**
1/2 cup (125 mL) dark brown sugar	**1/2 cup (125 mL) chocolate chips**
1¼ cups (310 mL) flour	**1/4 cup (60 mL) chopped nuts, of your choice**

Cream butter and sugar. Add flour and salt. Stir until well mixed. Place evenly in an 8 x 8-inch (20 x 20 cm) dish. Microwave at HIGH 3 minutes.
Melt chips in a cup 30 to 40 seconds at HIGH. Spread on cooked biscuits. Sprinkle with finely chopped nuts. Cool. Cut into bars.

Spiced Cookies In-A-Hurry

When your time is limited, try these. They are blended, dropped on waxed paper, chilled and ready to eat!

1/2 cup (125 mL) butter or margarine	1/4 tsp. (1 mL) salt
1/2 cup (125 mL) milk	1 tsp. (5 mL) vanilla or almond extract
2 cups (500 mL) sugar	1/2 cup (125 mL) peanut butter
1/4 cup (60 mL) unsweetened cocoa	3 cups (750 mL) quick-cooking oatmeal

Place in a bowl the butter or margarine and milk. Microwave 1 minute at HIGH. Stir and add sugar, cocoa and salt. Microwave 4 minutes at HIGH. Stir well, microwave 1 more minute at HIGH. Add vanilla or almond extract and peanut butter. Stir until well mixed. Add the oatmeal. Stir well and drop by teaspoons on waxed paper or cookie sheet. Refrigerate 1 to 2 hours.

Butter Crunch Cookies

This recipe will give you 4 to 5 dozen health cookies, and very easy to make.

3/4 cup (190 mL) butter or margarine	1/2 tsp. (2 mL) baking powder
3/4 cup (190 mL) sugar	1/4 tsp. (1 mL) salt
1 egg	1/2 cup (125 mL) oatmeal
1 tsp. (5 mL) almond extract	1/2 cup (125 mL) Grape Nut cereal
1½ cups (375 mL) flour	

Cream the butter or margarine. Gradually add the sugar. When well mixed, add the egg and almond extract. Mix thoroughly.
Sift together the flour, baking powder and salt. Add to first mixture. Mix and add the oatmeal and Grape Nut. Mix thoroughly. Shape into small balls. Place well apart on waxed paper set on a cardboard. Flatten each cookie with the bottom of a floured glass. Do not place too close as they spread. Microwave 4 to 5 minutes at MEDIUM-HIGH. Check doneness, remove cookies from the paper by sliding them off. Repeat for the remaining cookies.

Tea-time Currant Dainties (photo opposite p. 80)
(Convection or Microwave)

Dainty cookies, nice to serve at tea time. Cooked in the convection part of the microwave oven, they will be a deeper golden color. When in a hurry, I microwave them.

1/2 cup (125 mL) butter	Grated rind of 1/2 an orange
1/2 cup (125 mL) sugar	2 cups (500 mL) flour
3 eggs	1/3 cup (80 mL) currants

Cream butter until very soft, add the sugar and beat again, add the eggs and beat the whole 1 or 2 minutes with an egg beater, add the orange rind, then fold in the flour and the currants. Beat until thoroughly mixed.
Drop cookies on the prepared pan.* Microwave 3 to 4 minutes at MEDIUM-HIGH. Do not overcook, as they will be hard when cooled.
By the Convection Method: Preheat convection part of your microwave oven 5 minutes at 350°F. (180°C). Place cookies on a sheet that will fit into your oven. Bake 12 to 14 minutes.

A stiff cardboard topped with waxed paper makes a good cookie sheet for the microwave oven.

Lemon Pecan Dainties
(Convection)

An elegant tea time cookie!

3/4 cup (190 mL) butter	2 cups (500 mL) all-purpose flour
1 cup (250 mL) sugar	1 tsp. (5 mL) baking powder
1 egg	1/2 tsp. (2 mL) salt
Grated rind of 1 lemon	1/4 tsp. (1 mL) mace or nutmeg
1 tbsp. (15 mL) lemon juice	3/4 cup (190 mL) chopped pecans or walnuts

Cream the butter with the sugar, then add the egg, lemon rind and juice.
Combine dry ingredients and add to the creamed mixture. Mix well. Stir in pecans or walnuts.
Shape into rolls. Wrap in waxed paper and chill 6 to 24 hours. Slice thinly and place on ungreased baking sheet.
Preheat convection part of microwave oven to 375°F. (190°C) 15 minutes. Bake 10 minutes or until golden brown.

Jam Squares   (photo opposite p. 81, bottom right)

If you have bits of jam here and there, this is a good way to use them up, as you need only half a cup. I often mix jam, jelly and marmalade or I use any one type; no matter which the squares will be nice and tasty.

1/4 cup (60 mL) margarine

1/4 cup (60 mL) sugar

1 egg

1/2 cup (125 mL) flour

Grated rind of 1/2 a lemon

1/4 cup (60 mL) chopped nuts of your choice

1/4 tsp. (1 mL) cinnamon

A good pinch of salt

1/2 cup (125 mL) strawberry or raspberry jam

Topping:

1/2 cup (125 mL) flour

1/4 cup (60 mL) brown sugar

3 tbsp. (50 mL) butter or margarine

Beat the margarine and sugar until creamy. Add the egg, flour, lemon rind, nuts, cinnamon and salt. Mix until well blended.

Pour into an 8 x 8-inch (20 x 20 cm) baking dish. Microwave 4 to 5 minutes at HIGH, or until the middle part is slightly firm. Let stand 10 minutes. Spread top of cooked cake with the jam.

Mix the topping ingredients until granulated. Sprinkle evenly over the jam. Microwave 3 minutes at HIGH. Cool on rack. Cut into squares or bars. Enjoy!

Youngsters' Delight

And good for them, as they are made with grated carrots. Quick and easy to prepare.

1/2 cup (125 mL) margarine

1 cup (250 mL) well packed dark brown sugar

2 eggs

1 cup (250 mL) flour

1 tsp. (5 mL) baking powder

1 tsp. (5 mL) cinnamon

1/4 tsp. (1 mL) salt

1½ cups (375 mL) peeled and grated carrots

Place margarine in a bowl. Melt 2 minutes at HIGH. Add the brown sugar and the eggs, stir until well mixed. Stir together the flour, baking powder, cinnamon and salt. Add to creamed mixture, stir until well mixed. Add the grated carrots. Stir until well mixed in the batter.

Grease an 8 x 8-inch (20 x 20 cm) square dish. Pour prepared mixture into it. Microwave 8 minutes at MEDIUM-HIGH, check doneness with the point of a knife. If necessary, microwave another minute. Let stand 15 minutes on kitchen counter. To serve, cut into squares. Covered with foil, they will keep fresh 4 to 6 days.

Chocolate Brownies

I sometimes top these with thinly rolled almond paste. Super delicious. As almond paste is not readily available and somewhat costly, the brownies are also very nice without the almond paste.

1/3 cup (80 mL) shortening

2 ounces (56 g) unsweetened chocolate

1 cup (250 mL) sugar

3/4 cup (190 mL) flour

1/2 tsp. (2 mL) baking powder

1/2 tsp. (2 mL) salt

2 eggs

1/3 cup (80 mL) thinly sliced almonds

Place shortening and chocolate in an 8 x 8-inch (20 x 20 cm) Pyrex or Corning dish. Microwave 3 minutes at MEDIUM-HIGH, or until chocolate is melted. Add the remaining ingredients, stir well. Spread batter evenly in the baking dish.
Microwave 4 minutes at MEDIUM. Check doneness with a toothpick. If necessary, microwave another minute at MEDIUM-HIGH. Cool, cut into bars or squares.

Swiss Chocolate Squares

Swiss and chocolate are two inseparable words, and it is super good chocolate! Try these squares, you will enjoy them, and as a plus they are good keepers, if you hide them.

1/2 cup (125 mL) butter

3 tbsp. (50 mL) pure cocoa

1 cup (250 mL) sugar

2 large eggs

1 tsp. (5 mL) vanilla

3/4 cup (190 mL) flour

1 tsp. (5 mL) baking powder

1 cup (250 mL) slivered almonds or
  chopped walnuts

1 Swiss chocolate bar of your choice
  (use a bar of about 3½ oz or 100 g)

Grease an 8 x 8-inch (20 x 20 cm) Pyrex or Corning baking dish with shortening. Place the butter in a bowl, microwave 1 minute at HIGH. To this melted butter, add the cocoa, sugar, eggs and vanilla. Stir until well mixed.
Mix flour and baking powder. Add to first mixture. Add the nuts of your choice. Stir the whole to blend thoroughly.
Pour batter into the prepared dish. Spread evenly with a knife. Microwave 8 to 9 minutes at MEDIUM-HIGH. Test doneness with the point of a knife. If necessary, give it 30 to 40 seconds more.
Break the chocolate bar into pieces and place evenly over the surface of the baked squares. Cover pan and let stand on kitchen counter for 8 to 12 minutes, then smooth melted chocolate on top of the squares. Cool about 1 hour before cutting into bars or squares.

Carrot and Pineapple "Petits Fours" (photo opposite p. 81, left)

I make these in paper cups placed in a microwave-safe muffin pan. To taste, I cover them with frosting or simply sprinkle icing sugar over them. They may also be microwaved in small Pyrex cups.

1⅓ cups (330 mL) flour	1 cup (250 mL) carrots, finely grated
1 cup (250 mL) sugar	1/2 cup (125 mL) vegetable oil
1 tsp. (5 mL) cinnamon	1/2 cup (125 mL) crushed pineapple, well drained
3/4 tsp. (3 mL) soda	
1/2 tsp. (2 mL) salt	2 eggs
1/2 tsp. (2 mL) nutmeg	1/4 cup (60 mL) chopped nuts (optional)

Mix together the flour, sugar, cinnamon, soda, salt and nutmeg. Add the remaining ingredients and mix thoroughly.

Pour the batter either into paper cups placed in a muffin pan or into small Pyrex cups placed in a circle in the microwave. Microwave 2 minutes at HIGH. If your oven does not have a turntable, give the pan or the cups half a turn midway through the cooking. Microwave 1 minute at HIGH. It happens that the top of one or two of the "petits fours" may seem soft. Do not microwave further, the cooking will continue during standing time. Let stand 2 minutes on the kitchen counter, then unmold and place on a rack. Ice to your taste or sprinkle with icing sugar.

Helpful Hint

To remove cooking odor from microwave oven, mix in a bowl the juice and peel of half a lemon with a little water. Microwave 5 minutes at HIGH, then wipe the interior with a damp cloth.

Chocolate Bark (photo opposite p. 97, bottom right)

A microwaved sweet made in 5 minutes, ready to be served in ten.

1 package (350 g) semi-sweet chocolate chips	**3/4 cup (190 mL) chopped nuts of your choice**
1 tbsp. (15 mL) butter	**1/2 cup (125 mL) raisins**

Place the chocolate chips and the butter in a bowl. Microwave 4 minutes at MEDIUM-HIGH, stirring once.
When all the chips have melted, add the nuts and raisins, stir and spread on a piece of waxed paper set on a cookie sheet. Cool on kitchen counter.
To serve, break up in pieces.
Will keep 2 to 3 weeks in covered box in a cool place.

Nanaimo Bars (photo opposite p. 96)

In the 70's everyone was cooking these, which they called a cookie or a candy bar. To me, they are candy. Quick, easy to make and delicious.

1/2 cup (125 mL) butter or margarine	**2 cups (500 mL) graham cracker crumbs**
5 tbsp. (75 mL) sugar	**1 cup (250 mL) coconut**
5 tbsp. (75 mL) unsweetened cocoa	**1/2 cup (125 mL) chopped walnuts**
1 egg	**1/2 cup (125 mL) chocolate chips**
1 tsp. (5 mL) vanilla	

Melt butter or margarine in bowl, 1 minute at HIGH. Add sugar, cocoa, egg and vanilla. Stir until very well mixed. Add graham cracker crumbs, coconut and walnuts. Stir until well mixed. Pour into an ungreased 8 x 8-inch (20 x 20 cm) square pan. Spread equally. Wet your hands and press batter into pan. Sprinkle chocolate chips over all. Microwave 2 minutes at MEDIUM. Cool. Cover with plastic wrap. Refrigerate at least 1 hour or overnight. Cut into squares. Serve.

Granola Bars

Making your own is more economical and surely better in flavor. They will keep in a well covered container for 6 to 8 months. Serve as a cereal or make your own healthy sweets.

Homemade Granola:

4 cups (1 L) oatmeal

1 cup (250 mL) coconut

3/4 cup (190 mL) wheat germ

1/2 cup (125 mL) sesame seeds

1/2 cup (125 mL) chopped nuts of your choice

1/2 cup (125 mL) brown sugar

1/2 cup (125 mL) honey

1/2 cup (125 mL) margarine or butter, melted

1/2 tsp. (2 mL) salt

1 tsp. (5 mL) vanilla

1/2 cup (125 mL) raisins

Blend all the ingredients together, except the raisins, in a large glass bowl. Microwave at HIGH 10 minutes, or until the ingredients are toasted, stirring every 4 minutes. Stir in the raisins at the last 2 minutes of cooking. Cool, sprinkled on cookie sheet. Store in covered container. Yield: 6 cups (1.5 L).

Granola Bars:

1/4 cup (60 mL) sesame seeds

1/2 cup (125 mL) honey or corn syrup

3/4 cup (190 mL) chunky style peanut butter

3 cups (750 mL) homemade granola

1/2 cup (125 mL) chopped nuts of your choice

1/3 cup (80 mL) chopped dried apricots

1/4 cup (60 mL) sunflower seeds (optional)

1/4 cup (60 mL) wheat germ

Spread the sesame seeds in a baking dish. Microwave at HIGH 4 to 5 minutes, or until golden brown, stirring often. Set aside.

Measure honey or corn syrup in a large glass bowl, cover with waxed paper or cover, microwave 1 minute at HIGH. Blend in the peanut butter, microwave 30 seconds at HIGH. Stir in the remaining ingredients and the toasted sesame seeds. Press evenly on a 7 x 11-inch (17.5 x 27.5 cm) cookie sheet. Cover. Refrigerate 40 to 60 minutes. Cut into bars.

Marshmallow Treats

1 8-oz (250 g) bag of marshmallows

1/4 cup (60 mL) butter or margarine

5 cups (1.25 L) Rice Krispies cereal

In a large microwave-safe dish combine the marshmallows and the butter or margarine, microwave 4 to 5 minutes at HIGH, stirring twice. Add the cereal and stir well to coat thoroughly with the marshmallow mixture.

Press into buttered dish. Cool and cut into squares.

Creamy, Speedy Frozen Ice Cream

Quick, easy to prepare with ingredients that can be on hand whenever needed.

15 large marshmallows

1 tbsp. (15 mL) milk

1 cup (250 mL) commercial sour cream

1 package (425 g) frozen strawberries

Place marshmallows and milk in a bowl, microwave 2 to 3 minutes at MEDIUM, stir. By then the marshmallows should be melted. Add the sour cream and the thawed out frozen strawberries, mix thoroughly, pour into a mold, cover and place in the freezer.

Strawberry Ice Cream

This ice cream is at its best when served immediately, but it can be stored in the freezer for several hours. You may also keep the ice cream frozen for as long as one week.

4 cups (1 L) fresh strawberries, washed and hulled*

3/4 cup (190 mL) icing sugar

3/4 cup (190 mL) whipping cream

1 tbsp. (15 mL) orange liqueur (optional) or grated rind of 1 orange

At least five hours before serving, place strawberries on a baking sheet in a single layer and freeze until firm.
Just prior to serving, put frozen berries and icing sugar in the food processor or blender and chop finely. Without stopping, add the cream and orange liqueur or grated rind. Process until mixture is smooth and creamy, stopping several times to scrape.
When it has been kept in the freezer, process the ice cream for a minute until the mixture is smooth and creamy prior to serving.

* Frozen unsweetened strawberries may be substituted for fresh berries, in equal quantity.

Florentine Coffee Ice

Everyone in Florence seems to enjoy this delightful ice in the summer.

4 tbsp. (60 mL) instant coffee

2 cups (500 mL) water

1/4 to 1/2 cup (60 to 125 mL) sugar

1 tsp. (5 mL) vanilla

Combine in a bowl the instant coffee, water and the sugar, more or less to your taste. Microwave 5 minutes at HIGH, stir well. Microwave 2 minutes at HIGH. Cool and add the vanilla. Pour mixture into the ice tray or just place in the freezer and cool, stir well and freeze until firm.

To serve, pour the frozen coffee in a bowl, break up the pieces, let stand 5 to 10 minutes and beat with an electric beater until mixture is all broken up but still icy. It should have the consistency of a sherbet. Serve in small demi-tasses or glasses with a coffee spoon to eat it. If you so wish, it can be topped with whipped cream sweetened or plain.

Champagne Glass Granite (photo opposite p. 97, top right)

A Granite is a fruit flavored ice similar to a sherbet and most delectable. Following are my favorite mixtures.

For a very elegant dinner, serve it after the entrée and before the meat. "Very elegant Europe".

Lemon Granite

2 cups (500 mL) water

1 cup (250 mL) sugar

1 cup (250 mL) fresh lemon juice

Grated rind of 2 lemons

Orange Granite

2 cups (500 mL) water

3/4 cup (190 mL) sugar

1 cup (250 mL) fresh orange juice

Juice of 1 lemon

Grated rind of 1 orange

Strawberry Granite

1 cup (250 mL) water

1/2 cup (125 mL) sugar

2 cups (500 mL) mashed strawberries

2 tbsp. (30 mL) fresh lemon juice

Measure the water and sugar demanded by the chosen granite. Microwave at HIGH 5 minutes, stirring after 3 minutes of cooking. After the 5 minutes of cooking stir thoroughly and microwave again 3 minutes at HIGH. Cool the syrup.

Stir in the fruit juices or the fruit purée, according to the granite you are making. Pour mixture into a pudding dish (I use a deep pie plate) and freeze. While it is freezing stir every 30 minutes, scraping into the mixture all of the small ice particles that will first form around the edges.

When ready, the ice should have a fine, snowy texture. Serve in glasses or plates of your choice.

When you have made the ice the day before or early in the day, remove it from the freezer about 30 minutes before serving.

Sauces

Soft Custard Sauce

Serve with fresh fruit instead of cream or over cake or fruit cobblers.

2 cups (500 mL) milk	1/4 tsp. (1 mL) salt
1/3 cup (80 mL) sugar	3 eggs
1 tbsp. (15 mL) cornstarch	1 tsp. (5 mL) vanilla or almond extract

Measure milk in a 4-cup (1 L) glass measure. Add sugar, cornstarch, salt and eggs. Beat the whole with a rotary beater until smooth. Microwave at MEDIUM-HIGH 4 to 5 minutes, or until mixture begins to bubble, stirring twice during the last half of the cooking time. Microwave another minute or two at MEDIUM, if necessary. Stir in vanilla or almond extract. Beat until smooth with rotary beater. Serve warm or cold.

Tart Lemon Sauce

My favorite sauce for plum pudding and other types of steamed pudding.

1/2 cup (125 mL) butter or margarine	Grated rind of 1 orange
1 cup (250 mL) sugar	1 tbsp. (15 mL) water
1/4 cup (60 mL) fresh lemon juice	1 egg
Grated rind of 1/2 a lemon	

Place the butter or margarine in a bowl, microwave 1 minute at HIGH. Beat in the sugar, lemon juice, lemon and orange rind. Add the water and the egg, stir until well blended. Microwave 3 minutes at HIGH, stirring every minute. Cover, cool. As the sauce cools, it thickens. Serve cool or hot. Reheat 1 to 2 minutes at MEDIUM.

Butterscotch Sauce

An old-faschioned recipe which remains known for its flavor and its "finesse".

3 tbsp. (50 mL) all-purpose flour	2 or 3 tbsp. (30 or 50 mL) butter
1/2 cup (125 mL) dark or light brown sugar	1 tsp. (5 mL) vanilla extract
A pinch of salt	1/4 tsp. (1 mL) almond extract
1 cup (250 mL) cold water or light cream	

Place the flour, brown sugar and salt in a bowl. Mix well. Add the water or cream. Stir well. Microwave 3 minutes at HIGH. Stir and microwave 2 minutes more at "HIGH". Stir. The sauce is cooked when it is smooth and creamy. It may happen, if the ingredients were very cold, to have to microwave 2 more minutes at MEDIUM to finish the sauce. Add the butter, the vanilla and almond extracts and stir until the butter melts. Serve hot or at room temperature. This sauce may be kept from twelve to fifteen days in the refrigerator. It is easy to reheat the required quantity 1 to 2 minutes at HIGH, as needed.

Chocolate Chip Sauce

This sauce is flavored with cinnamon, but an equal quantity of nutmeg or ground cardamom or allspice added to it will vary the sauce without spoiling its quality. Serve warm over ice cream.

A 175-g package of chocolate chips*

3 tbsp. (50 mL) each water and milk

1 tsp. (5 mL) vanilla extract

1/2 tsp. (2 mL) allspice or cinnamon

Place in a bowl the chocolate chips, water and milk. Microwave 3 minutes at MEDIUM, stir well. If some of the chips are not melted, microwave another minute. Add the vanilla and the allspice or cinnamon. Stir until well mixed.

* Use milk or dark chocolate chips.

Hot Chocolate Sauce

The Dutch cocoa is the very best of all, but nowadays cocoa is expensive, so choose the one you wish, but do not use the sweetened cocoa for this super sauce.

1/2 cup (125 mL) pure unsweetened cocoa

1/2 cup (125 mL) sugar

1/4 tsp. (1 mL) salt

1 tbsp. (15 mL) cornstarch

1/4 cup (60 mL) corn syrup

1/4 cup (60 mL) heavy or light cream

1/4 tsp. (1 mL) vanilla extract

1/4 tsp. (1 mL) almond extract

Combine cocoa, sugar, salt and cornstarch in a bowl. Stir in the corn syrup and the cream. Microwave 3 to 5 minutes* at MEDIUM-HIGH, stirring twice. The sauce will become glossy and creamy. When tepid add vanilla and almond extract. Stir. Serve or let stand until cooled.** If the sauce has been refrigerated and if it is too thick, place at room temperature for 2 hours or warm up at MEDIUM 30 to 40 seconds.

* The time is difficult to determine exactly, as it depends on how cool the ingredients are.
** Sauce thickens quite a bit as it cools.

Rum Chocolate Sauce

Make a few days ahead of time, if you so wish. Pour into a glass dish or jam jar. When ready to serve, microwave, uncovered, 3 minutes at HIGH.

2 squares (1 oz - 28 g each) unsweetened chocolate

1/2 cup (125 mL) water

3/4 cup (190 mL) sugar

4 tbsp. (60 mL) butter

1/4 tsp. (1 mL) salt

2 tbsp. (30 mL) rum or
1 tsp. (5 mL) vanilla

Place chocolate and water in a glass 4-cup measure or a bowl. Microwave, uncovered, 3 minutes at HIGH. If chocolate has not melted completely, microwave another minute.
Add sugar, stir until well mixed with the chocolate. Microwave 2 to 3 minutes at MEDIUM. Add butter, salt, rum or vanilla. Stir and use.

Nanaimo Bars (p. 91) →

Best Hot Fudge Sauce

A super "not economical" fudge sauce which I adapted nine years ago to microwave cooking. One of the best sauces, yes, but to my surprise even better when made by the microwave method. Serve hot or tepid.

1/2 cup (125 mL) rich cream

3 tbsp. (50 mL) butter (unsalted, when possible)

1/3 cup (80 mL) white sugar

1/3 cup (80 mL) brown sugar

A good pinch of salt

1/2 cup (125 mL) cocoa

Place the cream and the butter in a bowl, microwave 4 minutes at MEDIUM-HIGH. Stir in the remaining ingredients and stir until well mixed. Microwave 4 minutes at MEDIUM-HIGH, stirring after 2 minutes of cooking.
Serve hot or at room temperature. It will keep 3 to 4 weeks refrigerated and well covered. Warm up what you require 1 to 2 minutes at MEDIUM.

Maple Pecan Sauce

Super sauce to serve over ice cream all year round, over bread pudding in the winter and over fresh strawberries in the summer.

2 tbsp. (30 mL) butter

1/4 cup (60 mL) water

3 tbsp. (50 mL) maple syrup

3/4 cup (190 mL) brown sugar

1/4 cup (60 mL) cream

1/4 cup (60 mL) pecans or walnuts

Place the butter in a bowl, microwave 2 minutes at HIGH, add the water, maple syrup and brown sugar. Stir well. Microwave 3 minutes at HIGH.
Add slowly, while beating, the cream and the pecans or walnuts. When I serve this sauce over fresh strawberries I omit the nuts, but I place a jug of cream on the table for everyone to use to taste. The sauce replaces the sugar on the berries.

← **To left:** Fresh Strawberry Glaze (p. 101)
← **Top right:** Champagne Glass Granite (p. 94)
← **Bottom left:** Raspberry or Strawberry Jam (p. 104) and
                Fine Shredded Marmalade (p. 107)
← **Bottom right:** Chocolate Bark (p. 91)

Melba Sauce

One of the tastiest dessert sauces. Will keep for 2 weeks covered and refrigerated.

A 10-oz (300 g) package frozen raspberries*
1/2 cup (125 mL) sugar
1 tbsp. (15 mL) cornstarch

1/2 cup (125 mL) currant or apple jelly
1 tsp. (5 mL) lemon juice
1 tbsp. (15 mL) brandy

Unwrap frozen raspberries, place in a 4-cup (1 L) dish.
Microwave, uncovered, 4 minutes at HIGH. Move the raspberries around, stir and break up, turn over and microwave another 2 minutes at HIGH. Blend the sugar and cornstarch. Stir into the raspberries, with the currant or apple jelly, lemon juice and brandy. Microwave at HIGH 4 minutes, stirring twice. When creamy, pour into a sieve, strain well to remove raspberry seeds and pour into an elegant serving dish. Serve hot or cold. To serve hot, reheat 1 minute at HIGH when ready.

* 2 to 3 cups (500 to 750 mL) fresh raspberries can replace the frozen raspberries. This does not vary the cooking period.

Orange Sauce

Rose water is more exotic than rum; it is also more difficult to find. Personally, I like to have a bottle of rose water on my flavorings shelf at all times. If you prefer to omit the rum or rose water, simply remove from the recipe, as the sauce is very well flavored with the orange rind and juice and the cloves.

1 tbsp. (15 mL) butter
1 tbsp. (15 mL) flour
3 whole cloves

Grated rind and juice of 2 oranges
2 tbsp. (30 mL) rum or
1 tsp. (5 mL) rose water

Melt the butter 1 minute at HIGH. Add the flour and stir. Add the remaining ingredients, stir and microwave 2 minutes at HIGH. Pour hot over peeled oranges, thinly sliced. Refrigerate.

Marshmallow Sauce

A light sauce that can be flavored according to your taste. Excellent over ice cream, sponge cake and creamy pudding.

1/4 cup (60 mL) water or cranberry juice
1/2 cup (125 mL) sugar
1/2 cup (125 mL) miniature marshmallows

1 egg white
1/2 tsp. (2 mL) vanilla extract or
1/4 tsp. (1 mL) almond extract

Place in a bowl, the water or cranberry juice and the sugar. Microwave 2 minutes at HIGH. Stir until sugar is completely dissolved, then microwave 2 minutes at HIGH, the mixture will then turn to a thin syrup. Add marshmallows and stir until they are melted. Set aside to cool.
Beat egg white until foamy. Gradually add to cooled mixture, stirring constantly. Flavor with the extract of your choice. This sauce will keep 4 to 6 days refrigerated. If it separates upon standing, simply give it a good stir before serving. It will regain its creamy consistency.

Superb Tart and Tangy Rhubarb Sauce

Serve cold with creamy dessert or ice cream, or fold in 1 cup (250 mL) sliced fresh strawberries in the sauce while hot.

4 cups (1 L) diced rhubarb

3 tsp. (15 mL) cornstarch

1 tsp. (5 mL) grated orange rind

1/4 tsp. (1 mL) nutmeg

1 cup (250 mL) sugar

1/2 cup (125 mL) fresh orange juice

Combine all the ingredients in a large glass mixing bowl. Stir thoroughly. Microwave at HIGH 8 to 9 minutes, or until mixture boils and thickens, stirring once or twice. Cool, then refrigerate.

Hot Blueberry Sauce

Hot over sponge cake, cold over ice cream, super! Add 2 peeled and thinly sliced apples, cook in the same manner, you will then have a delicious purple applesauce.

2 cups (500 mL) fresh blueberries

1/2 cup (125 mL) sugar

The grated rind of 1/2 a lemon

1 tbsp. (15 mL) lemon juice

1/2 cup (125 mL) water

1 tsp. (5 mL) cornstarch

2 tbsp. (30 mL) apple or orange juice

Place in a bowl, the blueberries, sugar, lemon juice, grated lemon rind and the water. Stir until well mixed. Microwave 4 minutes at HIGH. Stir and add the cornstarch mixed with the apple or orange juice. Stir and microwave 3 minutes at MEDIUM-HIGH. Stir after 2 minutes of cooking. The sauce is ready when it is creamy and glossy.

Rum Glaze

Pour over cake while it is still warm, any cake, white, sponge, chocolate, etc. It makes it moist and flavorful.

1/2 cup (125 mL) butter or margarine

1 cup (250 mL) sugar

Grated rind of 1/2 a lemon or 1/2 an orange

1/4 cup (60 mL) rum of your choice

Melt the butter or margarine in a 4-cup (1 L) measure 2 minutes at HIGH. Stir in the sugar, the grated lemon or orange rind and the rum. Mix well. Microwave 2 minutes at HIGH. Stir until sugar is all melted. Pour warm over warm unmolded cake.

Liqueur Glaze

Somewhat different in texture from the Rum Glaze. The type to use when you wish to have a special liqueur flavor.

1/2 cup (125 mL) butter or margarine

1/2 cup (125 mL) sugar

1/4 cup (60 mL) liqueur of your choice

1/4 cup (60 mL) water or apple juice

Melt the butter or margarine in a 4-cup (1 L) measure 2 minutes at HIGH. Add sugar, liqueur and water or apple juice. Microwave 2 minutes at HIGH, stirring after 1 minute of cooking.
Make slits here and there in the cake with a pointed knife and pour glaze over the cake. Let stand on a rack 2 to 3 hours before unmolding.

Super Chocolate Pecan Cake Frosting

I always enjoy this one on nut cakes. When the cake is made with walnuts, use walnuts, if there are pecans in the cake, use pecans, the quantity remains the same.

2 (1 oz - 28 g) squares semi-sweet chocolate

1/2 cup (125 mL) soft margarine

1 egg, beaten

1 tsp. (5 mL) fresh lemon juice

1½ cups (375 mL) icing sugar

1/2 cup (125 mL) chopped nuts of your choice

Place chocolate in a 4-cup (1 L) measure or in a bowl. Melt 1 minute 30 seconds at HIGH, stirring after 30 to 40 seconds. Add margarine and egg to hot chocolate. Mix thoroughly. Add lemon juice and icing sugar. Beat until creamy. Fold in the chopped nuts.
Frost cooled cake as soon as icing is ready.

Nutty Coconut Cake Topping

Frost cake with this crunchy topping when cake is unmolded but still hot.

1/2 cup (125 mL) nuts of your choice

1/2 cup (125 mL) coconut

1 cup (250 mL) brown sugar

1/2 cup (125 mL) rich cream or evaporated milk

1 tsp. (5 mL) vanilla extract

Place nuts and coconut in a 4-cup (1 L) bowl. Microwave 2 minutes at HIGH, stirring once. This will toast the coconut. Add brown sugar, milk or cream and vanilla. Mix until well blended. Spread on cake.

Fluffy Chocolate Cake Topping

Creamy, light, chocolate topping for any cake. There is no sugar in it, semi-sweet chocolate is used.

2 tbsp. (30 mL) hot water

1 tbsp. (15 mL) dry instant coffee

4 squares (1 oz each - 28 g) semi-sweet chocolate

1/4 cup (60 mL) whipping cream

Place the water in a bowl, microwave 1 minute at HIGH. Add the instant dry coffee, stir until well mixed, add the chocolate. Microwave 2 to 3 minutes at MEDIUM, stirring once. Cool mixture, whip the cream and fold into the cooled chocolate mixture. Fluff on top of a cooled cake.

Fresh Strawberry Glaze (photo opposite p. 97, top left)

The "glacé" is the French way of flavoring and topping cakes, mousse, fruit pies, fresh fruit, etc. It is beautiful to look at and very fragrant with the strawberry flavor.

4 cups (1 L) fresh strawberries

1 cup (250 mL) sugar

1 tbsp. (15 mL) cornstarch

1 tsp. (5 mL) grated lemon rind

1 tbsp. (15 mL) lemon juice

Crush 1½ cups (375 mL) of the strawberries with a fork, add the sugar, cornstarch, lemon rind and juice. Stir together until well blended. Microwave 3 minutes at HIGH, stirring 3 to 4 times. Pour hot over your chosen dessert.

Glazed Fresh Fruit

A quick and easy superlative dessert. Try it during the peak of the season for the fruit you have chosen, strawberries, raspberries, peaches or other.
Simply fill a dish with about 4 cups (1 L) of the fresh chosen fruit. Pour the warm strawberry glaze over, enough so the fruit will be completely covered and shiny.

Sliced Oranges in the Pink

Peel 4 to 6 oranges and slice as thinly as possible. Place them in a cut glass dish. Top with Fresh Strawberry Glaze (see above). Cover and leave overnight at room temperature and stir together just before serving.

Canned Pear Topping

A quick, attractive dessert, poured hot over ice cream or a square of lemon cake, or simply as is served in a small fruit dish.

2 tbsp. (30 mL) butter

1/3 cup (80 mL) brown sugar

1/4 tsp. (1 mL) each, cinnamon and nutmeg

1/4 tsp. (1 mL) ginger

1 large (28 oz - 796 mL) can pear halves*

Combine in a 9-inch (22.5 cm) microwave-safe pie plate, butter, brown sugar and spices. Microwave uncovered 2 minutes at MEDIUM-HIGH, stirring once. Drain pears, stir into the hot syrup and microwave, covered, 4 minutes at MEDIUM-HIGH. Serve as is or as suggested in caption.

* The pear halves may be sliced, to taste.

Jams in the Microwave

One day, facing an emergency that had to be dealt with immediately, I had a problem. I had just finished cleaning some strawberries to make jam. I knew it meant an hour of work. Suddenly, I happened to look at my microwave oven and said: "Why not?" Then and there I started to work "somewhat in the dark", and discovered I could make the jam, from fruit cleaning to jam-in-the-jar, in 30 minutes.

Really happy about it, I decided I would test more types of fruit, test cooking time, test keeping quality, etc. That was in 1982. At the end of that summer, I had a full shelf of all types of jams, labelled and waiting!

In 1985, I started to open some to sample flavor, color and keeping quality. I could not believe what I saw and tasted.

Whether I tried the 1982 or 1983 or 1984-1985, they were all fragrant, with perfect texture and flavor. "Never again, I said to myself, shall I ever make another jar of jam other than cooked in the microwave."

What is jam making

Jam making is transforming the fruit and its natural juices into a syrup. It is the personal touch that does give a special flavor to the jam.

How to sterilize the jars
- First, the jam jars must be sterilized.
- Uncover each jar, fill with hot or cold water.
- Place covers in a bowl, cover with hot or cold water. Place in the middle of the microwave oven.
- Place all the jars around the bowl — 6 to 8 jars is usually what is comfortable to use in any type of microwave oven.
- Microwave 20 minutes at HIGH. Using a cloth, as they are very hot, remove each jar to a tray, pull covers from the water, place on tray, cover the whole with a clean cloth. Repeat operation until all the jam jars you wish to use are sterilized. It does not matter if the water in the jars cools while waiting to be filled. What is important is to keep them covered with the cloth and empty the jars **only** when they are to be filled with the boiling hot jam or syrup and fruits.

Sterilize all the glasses you need before you start making the jam or preserve.

A few "How-to's" to remember
- Because microwaved jam relies on the natural pectin of the fruit with the help of the citric acid in the fresh lemon, these jams are lower in calories.
  Example: For most, 16 calories per tablespoon (15 mL) as compared with most commercial and old-fashioned jams which have about 50 calories per tablespoon (15 mL).
- Microwaved jams, made according to the following recipes, will keep 2 to 3 years in a cool, dark place, such as a cool pantry.
- Make sure all fruits are well washed before cooking them.
- When washing strawberries, raspberries, or any small soft fruits, do wash them before removing tails and wash as gently as possible under running cold water, with the fruit in a colander. Let them drain in the colander set over a tray. Remove tails when ready to make the jam.
- Do not double the recipes given for jam, the results will not be as perfect.
  The cooking period gives you just enough time to measure the sugar and prepare the fruit for the next batch.
- You need not wash the cooking pot between recipes, even if it is sort of sticky.
- The following recipes will give 5½ to 6 small 8-oz (250 mL) jars.

Raspberry or Strawberry Jam (photo opposite p. 97, bottom left)

Whether one or the other, it will cook in the same manner. I recommend using a small strawberry, such as the "Vercor type", for making jam, as they do not break up when cooking, and the big strawberries have less fragrance and are too much of a bite when used.

3 cups (750 mL) sugar

4 cups (1 L) strawberries or raspberries

Juice of 1/2 a lemon

Place sugar in a large microwave-safe bowl (12-cup - 3 L). Top with the strawberries or raspberries. Pour the lemon juice over all. Do not stir or cover. Microwave 10 minutes at HIGH. Stir thoroughly, all the sugar will be at the bottom of the bowl, and it must be well stirred with the fruits. Use a rubber spatula or a plastic spoon to stir so the fruits will not get crushed. Microwave uncovered another 10 minutes at HIGH.

Remove water from sterilized jars when you are ready to fill. Fill with the boiling jam, cover tightly without delay. Place filled jars upside-down on a cloth. Let stand 10 to 12 hours or until cold. Label, store. For your own information, mark the date.

Honeyed Peach Jam

Superb with hot croissants — but equally good served with roasted duck or quail. The fruit must be weighted for this jam, as size and texture of peaches vary quite a bit.

3 lb (1.5 kg) fresh peaches

2 inches (5 cm) cinnamon stick

1 tsp. (5 mL) whole cloves

1/2 tsp. (5 mL) allspice, whole or ground

2 cups (500 g) honey

3 tbsp. (50 mL) fresh lemon juice

1/4 cup (60 mL) fresh orange juice

1/4 cup (60 mL) hot water

1/4 tsp. (1 mL) salt

Pour boiling water over the peaches to cover then peel and pit them. Chop the peaches finely or pass through food processor for 2 seconds.

Tie loosely in a cheesecloth or a piece of cotton, the cinnamon stick and whole cloves and allspice. Place in the jam container with the peaches and the remaining ingredients. Microwave 10 minutes at HIGH. Stir well and microwave at HIGH 10 minutes more.

Depending on the maturity of the peaches, this jam sometimes needs 5 minutes more at HIGH, in the last part of the cooking. Bottle and cool as for the strawberry jam.

Autumn Plum Jam

No need to remove plum stones, as they will float to the top when jam is cooked. They are then easy to remove. The fresh mint leaves are at their best when those fragrant little blue plums are at the market in the fall.

Serve this deep purple jam with roast lamb or chicken, use to sweeten your fruit salads, a treat served with cottage cheese and toasted English muffins, in other words a "must" in your fruit cupboard.

1½ lb (750 g) blue autumn plums*

1 lb (500 g) sour or wild apples, sliced or chopped

4 cups (1 L) sugar

1 cup (250 mL) fresh mint leaves

Wash plums and cut around them, do not peel. Wash apples, peel and remove cores.
Place sugar in a large bowl, add the fruit and top with the mint leaves. Microwave, uncovered, 15 minutes at HIGH. Stir well. Microwave 10 minutes at HIGH, stir and microwave 10 minutes at MEDIUM. Pour into the sterilized jars, as given for the strawberry jam.

The stones are easily removed from the jam when it is cooked.

Green Apple Jam

This original old fashioned apple jam was given to me by my grandmother who inherited it from her mother. I hope today's mothers will give favorite recipes to their daughters who could later talk about them.

This jam was made with the first green apples appearing on the trees or at the market. Adapted to microwave cooking it turned out perfectly, with an even better color and flavor.

4 cups (1 L) unpeeled, chopped green apples

4 cups (1 L) first young rhubarb, diced

1 cup (250 mL) canned crushed pineapple, drained

1 cup (250 mL) seedless raisins or currants

Grated rind and juice of 1 orange and 1 lemon

4 cups (1 L) sugar

1/2 tsp. (2 mL) salt

1/2 tsp. (2 mL) each nutmeg and allspice

1/4 cup (60 mL) of the drained pineapple juice

Place all the ingredients in a large bowl. Stir well and let stand overnight on the kitchen counter. Microwave 15 minutes at HIGH, stir well and microwave 10 minutes at HIGH. Pour while hot into sterilized jam jars. Cover, turn upside down on counter. Let cool 10 to 12 hours.

Old-Fashioned Gooseberry Jam

Gooseberries and apples were a must in jam making in the 20's. Whenever I can find gooseberries, I hurry to make this tasty jam, which of course I adapted to microwave cooking with great ease and improved color and flavor, although I sincerely thought the old way could never be improved.

1¼ lb (625 g) gooseberries*

3 large apples

3 cups (750 mL) sugar

The juice of 1 lemon

Clean the gooseberries by removing the small tails and wash. Mash with a potato masher or pass through a food processor. Sprinkle with half the sugar. Cover with a cloth and let stand on the kitchen counter for 12 hours.

Peel, core and dice the apples and mix thoroughly with the gooseberries. Place in a large dish with the sugar and lemon juice. Microwave 10 minutes at HIGH. Stir well and microwave another 10 minutes at HIGH. Stir, pour into the sterilized jars. Cover and let stand 12 hours, upside down, on a tray or on the kitchen counter.

* Red or green gooseberries are equally good.

Dutch Pumpkin Jam

An autumn jam. Mother would sometimes use some of the Halloween pumpkin. For perfect results with this one, please use a scale.

2 lb (1 kg) pumpkin, peeled and diced*

3 cups (750 mL) sugar

1 tsp. (5 mL) fresh ginger root, grated

1/4 tsp. (1 mL) allspice

Grated peel of 1 lemon

Juice of 1 lemon

1/2 cup (125 mL) sweet Dutch Gin**

Peel and remove seeds from pumpkin, then weigh the 2 pounds (1 kg). Place in the microwave jam cooking bowl, in alternate layers, the sugar and the pumpkin. Cover with a cloth and let stand 24 hours in a cool place.

To cook, add the remaining ingredients to the pumpkin, except the gin. Microwave 10 minutes at HIGH. Stir well and microwave 10 minutes more at HIGH. Stir, add the gin, and microwave 10 minutes at MEDIUM. Stir well and pour into the sterilized jars. Cover. Let cool 12 hours, upside down.

 * Weigh the pumpkin after it has been peeled and diced.
** The best Dutch Gin for this jam is the ''De Kuyper''.

Fine Shredded Marmalade (photo opposite p. 97, bottom left)

I have microwaved this marmalade for the last four years and never lost a jar.

1 orange	Water
1 grapefruit	Sugar
1 lemon	

Remove rind of well washed orange, grapefruit and lemon with zester knife, in very small shreds, without any of the white part. Cover rind with boiling water, microwave at HIGH 5 minutes. Drain water. Cut fruit into very thin slices, discarding seeds. Add slices to peel, and measure.
Place the whole in a large bowl, add 1/4 cup (60 mL) of water for each cup of fruit. Microwave at HIGH 20 minutes. Add 1 cup (250 mL) of sugar for each cup of fruit mixture. Microwave at HIGH 15 to 20 minutes or until thick and amber colored. Stir a few times. Cool 5 minutes. Pour into hot sterilized jars. Cover and invert jars, leave 12 hours or more before labelling. Keep in a cool dark place.

Apple Rum Chutney

Every year I make this chutney. Since the older it gets, the better it is, be sure to date it. I have some that is seven years old.

5 cups (1.25 L) apples, pared, cored and chopped	2 tbsp. (30 mL) candied ginger
1 lemon, seeded and chopped	1½ tsp. (7 mL) salt
1 cup (250 mL) brown sugar	1/2 tsp. (2 mL) dried red pepper
1 cup (250 mL) granulated sugar	1 cup (250 mL) cider vinegar or Japanese vinegar
1½ cups (375 mL) seedless raisins	1/2 cup (125 mL) dark rum

Combine in a large saucepan the above ingredients, cover and microwave for 10 minutes at HIGH. Stir well, microwave at HIGH 10 to 15 minutes, or until thick and syrupy. Let stand 15 minutes, bottle, cover and invert the jars. Let stand 12 hours to cool.

Syrup for Frozen Fresh Fruit

For the last six years I have prepared all varieties of fruit for freezing, to enjoy through the winter months.

Thin syrup:
2 cups (500 mL) sugar
4 cups (1 L) water

Microwave 12 minutes at HIGH

Medium Syrup:
3 cups (750 mL) sugar
4 cups (1 L) water

Microwave 14 minutes at HIGH

Heavy Syrup:
5 cups (1.25 L) sugar
4 cups (1 L) water

Microwave 17 minutes at HIGH

Place in a large bowl (to prevent syrup from boiling over), the sugar and the water. Stir well after 6 minutes of cooking. The syrup must cool before adding the fruit.
Place prepared fruit, such as peeled peaches cut in half, in jars, with one hard stone in every jar. Top with the cooled syrup. Cover, label and freeze.

General Index

Printed by
PAYETTE & SIMMS, INC.
in August, 1986
at Saint-Lambert, Qué.